PIANO DANCE

PIANO DANCE

Extraordinary People, Places, and Pianos

NED KLEIN

TABLE OF CONTENTS

INTRODUCTION

FEW OCCUPATIONS ALLOW ONE TO MEET
and spend time with numerous interesting and accomplished people. While tuning and repairing pianos for over forty years, I have had a career that has been rich in amazing experiences and delightful surprises. I have been able to meet a wide range of people, from famous composers and performers to homeowners and their families. In addition, I have been able to work in places that the public rarely gets to see, from movie sets and concert hall stages, to some of the most luxurious homes in the nation.

Because I often spend several hours with people in their homes, they are frequently willing to tell me touching stories of their lives. In this collection of stories, I have recorded some of the more intriguing and varied stories of the people I have had the pleasure of meeting.

Also, I have found that pianists often become more interested in practicing and learning to play the piano when they are given the opportunity to learn more about how a piano works. For this reason, I enjoy taking the time to explain piano design and function to my clients and their children. In that spirit, I have included some sections of this volume to explain the mechanisms of pianos and the challenges of servicing them.

In piano work, the goal is to make the piano "sing." That is, by careful preparation to make the piano so sensitive and responsive that the performer can play a melody as though the instrument were singing. In response to that, I have a saying: "Lots of people can make a piano sing. My goal is to make one dance." In fact, in each of these stories you will find a piano taking a prominent role in the dance of life for each of these people. We often think of music as being peripheral to the important things in life. Much to the contrary, I feel that music is an essential element of a meaningful life.

I hope you enjoy these stories, and I hope that they enhance your interest in this remarkable instrument.

IT ALL STARTED WITH A MUSIC TEACHER

M R. LOUIS GRUBB CARRIED HIMSELF WITH an air of dignity and self-confidence. I studied singing with him in the 1960's and 70's. He had been assistant conductor of the Philadelphia Opera in the 1920's, and he had worked with some of the greatest singers of that era. He knew singing and voices, and he could play virtually anything on the piano by ear or by memory. Somehow he had ended up teaching private music lessons in Delaware, a relative cultural backwater. He was always a little disgruntled about it, but he loved to hunt ducks in the Delaware estuaries.

To help pay the bills, he played organ at a small rural church for decades. He loved to tell me about a committee chairman approaching him one day to say that some of the congregation were concerned to see him playing the whole service every week without any music on the music rack of the organ. Mr. Grubb told me that he quieted their fears by putting a single piece of sheet music upside-down on the music rack and leaving it there for years, while he continued to play without written music.

It wasn't until years later, when I studied singing with various teachers in Boston, that I realized that it is almost unheard of for a voice teacher to be able to play piano adequately. Almost all voice teachers are retired singers and they usually need to hire a pianist to accompany lessons. That additional cost for the accompanist gets passed on to the students. Mr. Grubb did not just play adequately, he played extraordinarily well. For example, he always accompanied his students at their recitals.

His skill at the piano makes sense when you think of his background as an assistant conductor of the opera. His job included urgent training of replacements. If a singer lost their voice or got sick, it was his job to train someone quickly to take over a role. He told of one instance that occurred while an opera was being performed, and a singer with a minor role was suddenly too sick to perform. Mr. Grubb chose a smart young woman from the chorus and took her to the practice room. Using the piano and playing by memory, he taught her the cues, words, and music as fast as she could learn them. When she asked why they were doing that, he refused to tell her, so she would not get nervous. As soon as she learned the role, he accompanied her up to the wings, where the opera was in mid-performance. By that time, she had figured out that she was going onstage momentarily. He gave her some words of encouragement and when it was time for her entrance, he gave her a gentle push onto the stage.

Prior to my studying with Mr. Grubb, he had taught my mother for several years. He taught the singing technique of "the great Bernardo DeMuro," an Italian tenor who toured the US in the 1920's. His motto was, "A great back is a great voice." The theory was that the back muscles could be used to stabilize the diaphragm, so that the neck muscles could be free of tension and allow the voice to "float" freely and without restriction. My mother sang noticeably better under Mr. Grubb's instruction. She sang lead roles in local amateur productions and she sang solos in church. She had also sung as a soloist with an amateur group on New York radio in the 30's and 40's. I've had a chance as an adult to be around some of the best voices, and hers was unusually good. I have always had a good ear for voices, and I owe that gift to my mother. It's no wonder, because it is well accepted now that children are listening, even in the womb. By checking the date of a 78 rpm recording that I have of my mother singing "The Lord's Prayer" on the radio, I determined that at the time of the recording she was pregnant with me. She practiced singing every day, and she always took her performing very seriously. She told me that when I was a toddler, I would sing the tune of songs along with her before I could say words.

I studied singing with Mr. Grubb when I was in high school and then after college when I was back at home. He also taught some of his other students in my mother's studio a couple afternoons a week. Instead of paying rent to my mother for the use of her studio, he gave both of us free singing lessons. He had also taught my mother how to teach piano. She played piano well, but she did not have a degree in music. He explained that a degree was not necessary to teach beginning piano lessons for children. He taught my mother which piano lesson books to use and how to teach effectively. She was very good with children, so she regularly had a full schedule of students.

As a result, she was able to put me through college with her piano teaching.

Going immediately from high school to college without interruption was crucial in those days, because young men who lost their college deferments were sent off to the Vietnam War. As we all know, even the ones who came back were often never the same. If it had not been for Mr. Grubb, all of our lives could have been a lot more difficult. During my teenage years, my father became disabled with advanced multiple sclerosis, and he could no longer work. By teaching at home, my mother was able to be around the house whenever my father needed her, and at the same time she could still make a living. This was remarkably fortuitous for our family.

At college, I majored in anthropology, specializing in archaeology, which is not a very marketable degree. After college, I was staying with my parents and making a little money waiting tables and performing in dinner theater productions. Mr. Grubb helped me improve my singing, but he was always honest about my lack of professional level talent. I have a very good ear, but not a great voice. We were discussing my future during one lesson, and Mr. Grubb suggested that I look into becoming a piano tuner. He said his piano tuner did fairly well financially and since he was able to arrange his own schedule, it allowed a lot of flexibility for other activities. This could enable me to perform as much as I wanted and still earn a living. I investigated what it would take to become a piano tuner, and I decided that it was the profession that I wanted to pursue.

So far, I have had an extremely enjoyable career tuning pianos for over forty years. I have always been grateful to Mr. Grubb for suggesting that I become a piano technician. After having worked in the field for just a few years, I visited Mr. Grubb at his retirement home in Camden, Maine. I thanked him again for leading me in this direction.

Mr. Grubb had a rich and full life. He had a pleasant marriage with children, and he and his wife had long and happy lives together. He had many talented and creative friends, and he got to retire to a beautiful place. He taught hundreds of music students both singing and piano, and as a result of his talent and inspiration, his students in turn have touched the lives of thousands of people.

For me, Mr. Grubb made a particularly great contribution to my life and happiness. Not only have I had an enjoyable and worthwhile career as a piano tuner, I have had amazing opportunities to perform as an amateur. Most amateur musicians struggle with taking time off work in order to perform. Luckily that was never an issue for me, since piano tuning gave me the scheduling flexibility that few occupations allow. As an added benefit, wherever I performed it seemed that I was able to get more piano work from all of the musicians I met. Over the years, some of the opportunities I have had include singing in the chorus that performs with the Boston Symphony Orchestra at Symphony Hall and at Tanglewood, going on tour with the symphony to sing at Carnegie Hall and Lincoln Center, and appearing on TV reruns for years in *Arthur Fiedler's Christmas at Pops*. Additionally, I have had roles in several community productions of musical comedies. In short, I have been very fortunate that piano tuning and music performance have made such a large contribution to the quality of my life.

PIANO TUNING SCHOOL AND THE VENDOME FIRE

NORTH BENNET SCHOOL OF BOSTON HAD a different name in the 1970's, when I attended the school to learn piano tuning. It was called North Bennet Street *Industrial* School. That name was left over from a previous era when the school prepared boys for the trades, rather than for academic work. In addition to offering instruction in piano tuning, the school offered courses in trades such as jewelry repair, preservation carpentry, violin making, bookbinding, and several other crafts.

When I attended, the piano technology course was six months long, and it was offered twice a year. My class in piano technology had twelve students and one instructor, William Garlick. He was English and was a graduate of the London School of Furniture, which was the piano technology school in England. He had also attended North Bennet Street Industrial School and had taken over teaching at the school when the previous teachers retired.

The students were a varied group of people, and there

was quite an age range. For example, two students were as young as nineteen, and two were in their fifties. The class included only one woman, who was in her late twenties and had two children. Her husband drove a taxi at night and watched the children during the day so that she could attend school. While he took care of their children during the day, he was writing a novel about the 1960's student life at the University of California at Santa Barbara, where he and his wife had attended college together.

One of my older classmates, Jim, was a former steel worker who had been injured on the job, and was consequently being retrained for a new occupation. His injury took place while working on the steel framing for a large office building. Jim heard a yell and saw a fellow worker falling from the steel structure a few floors above him. Jim was strapped to the structure, so he was somehow able to reach out with both arms and catch the falling worker, saving his life. The force of the collision seriously injured Jim, however, so he was no longer able to do the physically demanding job of a steel worker. Jim was a generous man who always offered to buy lunch or snacks for the rest of us starving students who were pinching pennies.

After the first school day, two of my classmates and I decided to look for an apartment together. The school was located in the "North End" of Boston, right next to Old North Church, famous for the lanterns signaling Paul Revere's ride. The North End was an Italian neighborhood. While walking to school each day, we would pass meat markets with skinned rabbits hanging in the windows, and aromatic bakeries with a variety of Italian cookies. The streets were narrow, more like European streets than those in the U.S.

The nearest apartments for us to consider were on the north side of Beacon Hill, which was just a short walk away. Beacon Hill is known for its opulent historic homes, but there was a small section on the north side that contained some older apartment buildings with units that were cheap enough for students to afford. We could only afford a two-bedroom apartment for the three of us, but fortunately one of my roommates, Kendrick, offered to sleep in the living room. My other roommate, Maury, and I flipped a coin to determine who would get which bedroom. As it turned out, Maury got the back bedroom, and I got the front bedroom of the first floor apartment, where people passed by on the sidewalk right outside my window.

School days started at 8 am. Officially the school day ended at 2 pm, but Mr. Garlick was so committed to our success that he would often stay until as late as 8 pm for us to practice our tuning and repair skills. Six months was, after all, very little time to learn all that we needed to know in order to be independent technicians, so we were grateful to have the extra time to learn and practice each day. Nowadays the course has been lengthened to one year with an optional second year, for instruction in complete piano rebuilding. The new length of time is definitely more realistic. As a result, upon graduation most of the students these days are able to immediately pass a rigorous certification test given by the Piano Technicians Guild.

That certification test was instituted to help the public. Since piano tuning does not involve public safety, there are no government regulations or licensing. Because of this, anyone may call themselves a piano technician, whether or not they have any piano service skills. In order to help protect the public, a private organization called the Piano Technician's Guild, has created a series of very difficult exams covering piano tuning, repairs, and regulation, so as to ensure that the piano tuners they certify are competent technicians. There are fewer than 2,500 tuners who have passed the Piano Tuners Guild exam, and have the certification of *Registered Piano Technician*.

A typical school day would involve an hour or two of class instruction, and then we would all disperse to our practice rooms. Tuning was the most difficult skill of all to learn, so we each spent most of our time alone in a room practicing piano tuning. Mr. Garlick would make the rounds to each room to check our work and to assign us the next step of tuning on which to practice. Learning to tune is one of the most difficult things I have ever attempted.

My piano tuning course at North Bennet ran from March through August of 1972. When summertime began, Mr. Garlick organized voluntary outings one or two evenings a week for his students to go to the Hatch Shell (Boston's epicenter for large outdoor performances and open-air events) to hear the Boston Pops Orchestra play. The Hatch Shell is located on the esplanade near the Charles River, and the concerts were open to the public free of charge. A shell, of course, is shaped a little like a clam shell on edge, and the structure was constructed for amplifying sound for outdoor concerts. This one was constructed in 1941 by Maria Hatch, to honor her late brother, Edward Hatch, resulting in an ironic and memorable combination of words: *Hatch Shell*. We would all bring our blankets for the lawn and food for dinner, and we would lie out under the stars and listen to live light classical music. It was very enjoyable.

Arthur Fiedler, the Director of the Pops, had organized

these concerts during the Great Depression. The free concerts were a great gesture by the orchestra for a public that was experiencing hard times. It is also part of the reason that the people of Boston have great pride and affection for the orchestra, such as I have never seen in any other American city. Thousands of people still come to hear their concerts on weeknights during the summer months. It is a very pleasant experience to sit in the evening with hundreds of music lovers and listen to such beautiful music outdoors.

The biggest event, of course, was on the Fourth of July. Thousands of people crowded the esplanade (the park located next to the Charles River) beginning in the morning hours. The orchestra would play in the evening, climaxed by Tchaikovsky's *1812 Overture*, followed by a major display of fireworks set off from a barge on the river. The *1812 Overture* was written to honor the Russian victory over Napoleon, but Americans have adopted the music as representing our own victory over the British.

It's difficult to describe how moving it was to hear the finish of the *1812 Overture*, with church bells ringing all over the city and cannons firing. It was hard not to have tears in your eyes, imagining people celebrating their hard-fought victory over oppression. Several years later, I discovered that they no longer fire cannons at the end of the music. Instead, they use modern howitzers, which still fill the bill for lots of booming. It was absurdly coincidental, but I found out about the howitzers because I tuned the home piano for the officer of the National Guard who would give the orders to fire them on cue to the music. Is Boston a small town, or what?

After experiencing the crowds of the Fourth of July

concert, I had a greater appreciation for how pleasant it was to attend the weeknight concerts with only a few hundred people, which allowed plenty of room for us to lie down or walk around. One particular concert was very memorable to me. Here is the background of the story.

There was a large historic building, called the Hotel Vendome, that was undergoing renovation. It was a five-story structure, located at the corner of Commonwealth and Dartmouth in Back Bay, a fashionable and historic area of town near the esplanade. The Vendome was originally built in 1871 and expanded in 1882. In June of 1972, there were only a few workers inside when a fire broke out. A number of Boston fire companies battled the blaze for hours, before it was extinguished. Since the fire was in the afternoon, it was being watched by a large crowd of people, including a couple of my fellow students from the piano tuning school. After three hours, the fire appeared to be extinguished. Then without warning, all five stories of the southeast corner of the building collapsed on top of seventeen fire fighters, killing nine of them, as hundreds of people watched in horror. The rubble covered an entire ladder truck, leaving a two-story pile of debris. The cause of the collapse was later determined to have been the weight of four floors of water on a weakened steel beam. In terms of loss of life of the firefighters, it was the worst tragedy in the 300 years of Boston firefighting. Boston is more like a tight-knit community, than an impersonal city. The loss of those fire fighters was deeply felt by many people in the city.

The next evening there was another concert at the Hatch Shell, which was conducted by Arthur Fiedler himself. He was getting older and had been leading those concerts for more than forty years. Often the weeknight concerts would have a guest conductor in order to give Mr. Fiedler a break, but that evening he chose to conduct. For decades he had been a champion of the fire departments of Boston, creating many events for and with them. Years earlier they had made him an honorary fire chief, with his own red helmet that he wore proudly.

That evening at the Hatch Shell concert, Mr. Fielder asked the audience to rise to honor those men who had lost their lives fighting the Vendome fire. As we stood there, the orchestra played Aaron Copland's *Fanfare for the Common Man*. I had never heard it before and it took my breath away. If you're not familiar with this piece, the music was written in 1942 and is a fanfare for brass and percussion, extolling the infinite qualities in each of us, no matter what our social status might be. It was extraordinarily beautiful and appropriate. Hundreds of people stood together, sobbing and yet finding some type of comfort in the warm summer evening by the river as they listened to the beautiful tribute to those who gave "the last full measure of devotion" to their city and to its people.

Alfred Nash Patterson, Choral Conductor

AFTER GRADUATING FROM PIANO TUNING school, I decided to continue living in Boston. I started my first full-time job in October, 1972 at the Steinway franchise of Boston, located just across the street from the Boston Common, which is the central public park in downtown Boston. It was an exciting time for me since I was beginning my new occupation as a piano tuner. I worked in the piano shop repairing and rebuilding pianos, and sometimes I was sent out on jobs to troubleshoot problems with new pianos that had been recently delivered to private homes.

Singing was always an important part of my life, so I decided to join a large chorus. After going through a tough audition that included sight reading of some very difficult modern music, I was accepted into the Chorus Pro Musica of Boston, the premier choral group in Boston. My first performance with the chorus was Beethoven's *Ninth Symphony* with the Boston Symphony Orchestra. The choral section was to be performed from memory, so a great deal of practice was required outside of rehearsal time. I was also working 45 hours a week, so I did not have a lot of spare time. However, since my work at the piano store was more physical than mental in nature, I could often work on memorization of the German lyrics while I worked. I would just spread the music out on a Steinway soundboard, and then I would memorize the music as I fitted shims to the cracked soundboard. It was surprising how well that worked out for me.

We rehearsed the choral music on Monday nights for a couple months with our regular choral conductor, Alfred Nash Patterson. During the week that led up to the performances, we had two rehearsals with Bernard Haitink of the Royal Concertgebouw Orchestra of Amsterdam. Haitink had been hired as a guest conductor by the Boston Symphony, specifically for this performance. It was quite an experience for me as a young man to be part of such a big event. As an amateur musician, I was given the opportunity to sing with some of the greatest musicians in the world, performing one of the most important pieces of music ever written. This was something that was far beyond any of my expectations. It's very thrilling to walk out onto the stage of Symphony Hall to a packed audience. The hall seemed to be a block long, and glowed with its gold and ivory furnishings. We sat right behind the orchestra, so I was able to watch the instrumentalists up close as they played. The entire performance went extremely well, and it was an extraordinary experience to be part of.

Our choral conductor, Alfred Nash Patterson, was the original founder of the Chorus Pro Musica. He started the chorus in 1949 with a dream of creating a first rate organization to perform the most beautiful and most challenging choral music available. Many of the best amateur singers in Boston were drawn to him for his combination of skill, musicianship, great sense of humor, and warm personality. He had a rare gift of expressing a depth of beauty in music that I have not found since in any conductor. Many of the members of the chorus had sung with him for twenty years. He inspired that kind of loyalty and dedication. People in the chorus had shared rare experiences of beauty for decades, which made for some strong friendships.

A few weeks after the Beethoven concert, the chorus performed three Christmas concerts. One concert was for the Massachusetts governor at the State House rotunda, one was at the Harvard Club, and the third concert was held at Old South Church in Boston.

At the dress rehearsal for the last Christmas concert, Mr. Patterson approached me during a break. He knew I was a piano technician, and he told me that he was in a bit of a bind. His home piano had a problem which needed to be corrected by the following evening, because the entire chorus would be attending a party at his house. He explained that he had asked his usual piano tuner to make the piano action a little lighter to the touch, but after his work many of the notes would "cheat;" that is, when the key was played the hammer would not strike the string. Instead, there would be just a thudding sound of the key hitting bottom, but no sound of the string being struck. The piano was unusable in its present condition and the decades-long tradition was for the chorus to use the piano to accompany singing at the party. I explained to Mr. Patterson that I would be happy to help, but I didn't own a car to get out to his house, plus I had to work all the next day. The only way I could fix it would be to bring my tools to the concert and then to the party, as I was getting a ride with another chorus member.

The night of the party, I pulled out the piano action, which includes the keyboard and all the mechanism that moves the hammers up to the piano strings. While numerous people watched, I put the action up on top of the piano and analyzed the movement. For each note, there are ten major adjustments and many minor ones that must be correctly adjusted in order for each note to work. As it turned out, the previous technician hadn't fully understood how piano actions function. He had tightened the jack regulating buttons, disturbing the position of the jack under the knuckle. This is a crucial relationship for an action to work properly.

The work he had done would not have lightened the touch anyway, and the downside of his attempts was that many of the notes did not play. I adjusted the jacks properly in about half an hour, and the piano worked perfectly for the party. That evening in Boston was a remarkable opportunity for me as a piano tuner. About a hundred singers watched me work on Mr. Patterson's piano and they likely concluded that he respected the quality of my work. Most singers own a piano, and my career goal was to gradually build up my own clientele by tuning at night and on weekends, until I had enough business that I didn't have to work at the piano store any longer. The exposure that I got that night was a considerable start. Mr. Patterson had essentially jump-started my career with just one night's work, but following that job he did even more. For years to come, he found excuses to ask me a question about a piano in front of large groups of people whenever he could, so that everyone would know that I was his piano tuner. He almost single-handedly started my piano tuning business, and I have always been grateful.

Mr. Patterson was a delightful man to spend time with. Once or twice a year we would need to move a grand piano from the third floor of Old South Church down to the sanctuary for a concert, then move it back up again afterward. I would borrow the moving equipment from the piano store. With the help of a couple large volunteers from the chorus, we would put the piano on its side, pull off the legs and the lyre (pedal assembly), strap the piano onto a board, tip it onto a four-wheel dolly and wheel it over to the elevator. Mr. Patterson always wanted to be part of the team. The experience of moving a huge 1920's Mason & Hamlin piano is a little like being a child. The piano is so big that it makes you feel small again, somehow. That's the best explanation I can think of, because we always ended up laughing like children when we did it.

I enjoyed singing in the chorus for eleven years, and it was a great opportunity for me in many ways. I made numerous friendships with extraordinary people, and the concerts were always so beautiful that they were moving experiences. I had the chance to perform many major choral works with delightful people in spectacular concert halls all around the Boston area. To top it off, we had outstanding parties, where people would sing together for hours. One of the chorus members was a wealthy doctor who graciously invited us all to his summer house in New Hampshire every year for a party and a softball game. It was truly a great time in my life.

As the years went by, when Mr. Patterson was in his late sixties or early seventies, he had a heart attack. After having open heart surgery, he spent months recuperating. Our assistant conductor was leading the chorus during Mr. Patterson's recuperation, so I hadn't seen him for a few months. Then one day, on a break between tunings, I was walking in a park near his home in Newton, and I saw Mr. Patterson and his wife sitting on a bench talking together quietly. I was so excited to see him that I ran over and hugged him spontaneously without even thinking about it ahead of time. I'd never hugged him before, but I was so happy to see him that my affection for him just took over. I don't remember what was said, but we must have visited for a few minutes before I headed off.

Eventually he recovered enough to come back and lead a few chorus rehearsals, but then unfortunately he passed away suddenly. Some years later, I was tuning his home piano for his wife. She told me that he was very moved by my hugging him the way I had. She said that men simply didn't do that kind of thing in his day, and he appreciated it enormously. Remembering his appreciation for my affection is one of my fondest memories.

His funeral was a beautiful celebration of his life and work. The enormous Old South Church was standing room only. The entire chorus was there, along with many former members of the chorus, numerous musicians from the area, and music lovers from all over the city. There was also a volunteer orchestra of members of the Boston Philharmonic Orchestra. Hundreds of people brought their own music and we all sang portions of the Mozart *Requiem*, directed by Don Palumbo, who would become the new director of the Chorus Pro Musica. I found that singing with the chorus at an important real life event was a much more moving experience compared with singing at a concert. It was as though the concerts were just play-acting by comparison.

The reverence and appreciation that hundreds of musicians had for this man was immense and palpable. It was truly an honor to know such a wonderful man as Mr. Alfred Nash Patterson.

FLYING PIANOS

IN 1972, SOON AFTER I BEGAN WORKING AT the piano store in Boston, I answered a phone call that came into the shop. It was a Massachusetts Institute of Technology (MIT) student on the phone, inviting me and my coworkers to come over to Cambridge and watch them throw a piano off the roof of a dormitory. We were all too busy to go there on a moment's notice, so none of us saw it. For decades I wondered about it and regretted that I hadn't found a way to go see such an extraordinary and outrageous event take place.

My interest stemmed in part from an inaccurate belief that I had held since the start of my career. Some basic information about pianos will help to explain this. Pianos have over 200 strings at an average tension of 150 pounds. If you multiply 200 x 150, you get 30,000 pounds of total tension. In early pianos, just a few dozen strings at constant tension were enough to pull up the corners of the wooden instruments. It was called "going into wind," as in "to wind a clock." To keep pianos straight, cast iron plates were gradually developed to reinforce the structures. Nowadays, they are called "full" cast iron plates, as opposed to the "partial" ones prior to 1900. Cast iron is used because it bends very little, even under tremendous pressure. It can break, however.

Early on in my career, a more experienced tuner had told me it was possible that a plate could break in such a way that the piano would implode on itself, sending parts flying in all directions. As a result, I had believed that if a piano were dropped off the roof of a building, the piano plate would likely break when the piano hit the ground, resulting in a very spectacular and noisy implosion. For over thirty years I had wondered about that piano being thrown off the roof at MIT, and I had tried to imagine what it would have sounded like when it struck the ground.

Thirty-two years later, in 2004, my fiancée and I were visiting one of her childhood friends, Donna, in Santa Fe. Donna introduced her husband, Bill, who was about my age. Bill and I got to talking and discovered that we were both living in Boston in the early 70's. When Bill mentioned that he went to MIT, I had to ask him if he knew about the piano being thrown off the roof. He answered, "Yes, I was there." I couldn't believe my good fortune. After all those years, I suddenly had an opportunity for a first-hand account of the event. Here is my recollection of his story:

The event was organized by Charlie Bruno, who did it as a project for a class he was taking. He calculated ahead of time the volume of the hole the piano would make in the ground after it fell six stories. In the tradition of all great scientists, he named the volume of such a hole a "Bruno," after himself. Thus, a piano that's dropped six stories will result in one "Bruno." The piano was pushed off the roof of Baker House, a 6-story dormitory, and it landed in a back alley called Amherst Alley, creating the expected "Bruno." No more, and no less. I was very happy to finally know the exact details of the event.

Six years later, in 2010, as I was preparing to write this story, my fiancée suggested that I look up the event on the internet. For some reason, I had never thought of that. The world had changed a lot since 1972, but I guess not much of my thinking had changed, in terms of the use of the internet. When I typed in "Charlie Bruno MIT piano" on a search, I couldn't believe what I found. There are numerous articles about it and even a video to watch of the original event.

At the time, some of the MIT students were taking a high speed photography class, and they took videos of the drop, so that it could be played back in slow motion. The entire event has somehow reached mythic proportions. It is now an annual tradition at MIT, so you can view videos of other pianos being dropped in subsequent years, as well. It is considered to be an important event in the academic year, coinciding with the last day to *drop* classes. I thought I had narrowly missed a once-in-a-lifetime event from 38 years ago, but here it was available online in slow motion replay, any time that I wanted to see it.

The one thing missing for me, however, was a spectacular SPRONG and implosion that I had anticipated would happen when the piano struck the ground. You can hear a crash on the videos, but it was only slightly more than you would expect from such a large piece of furniture. When witnesses were interviewed on camera afterwards, they generally said that they were disappointed with the sound. Unfortunately, it seems that my belief about spectacular implosions was just wishful thinking.

There was another way, however, that I finally saw the

crash and heard the sound I was hoping for. During the 1990's, there was an episode of a television program called *Northern Exposure* where they appeared to fling a piano up in the air with a catapult. The flight of the piano was televised in slow motion, and it was staged so that the keys and various parts of the piano fell away as the piano seemingly flew through the air. The crash landing that was televised was very dramatic and the sound effects were spectacular. Although it was all staged and the sound was dubbed, I loved watching it anyway, since it conveyed the same type of dramatic sound and implosion that I had always envisioned.

THE FINEST
PIANO TUNER

B ARRY WAS THE BEST PIANO TUNER I EVER
knew. We both worked at Steinert's, the Steinway
franchise of Boston. At the time I met him, I had recently
graduated from tuning school, and he had already been
tuning for about five years. Occasionally I was asked to
tune a piano that Barry had previously tuned, and I could
tell how well he tuned by how little out of tune it was.

One of those occasions was at the recording studio for
WBGH, which was the public TV station in Boston. For
two days, they were recording a series of songs performed
by a well-known opera singer, with piano accompaniment.
Barry had tuned the studio's piano the first morning, and
they had recorded songs that day using the piano. WGBH
had paid our piano store for Barry to sit in the control
room all day long in case something went wrong with the
piano. Barry hated sitting there so much that he called in
sick the following day, so he wouldn't have to do it again.
That is how I got sent over on the morning of the second
day to tune the piano for that day's recording session.

When I arrived at the studio, I checked the piano that

Barry had tuned the day before, and I could not find a single string that could be improved. Never in my 43 years of tuning have I ever encountered that again. To give some perspective, for concerts a piano will often be tuned twice the day of the performance: once before the rehearsal and again right before the concert. For a piano to be tuned as well and as stably as Barry had tuned that piano is almost unheard of. Pianos go out of tune constantly, so the goal of a tuner is not just to tune accurately, but also to tune stably. Tuning stably is an additional skill that is harder to master than tuning accurately. There are several reasons it is difficult to tune stably. One is that tuning pins are not perfectly rigid. They both twist and bend. The pins are held firmly at the bottom in the piano, but are tuned by twisting the top of the pin with a tuning lever. If the piano tuner leaves a twist or a bend in the pin, the pin will gradually straighten over the next few minutes or hours, putting the piano out of tune. Another reason that stable tuning is difficult is that there are three portions of each string, but you can hear only the portion in the middle of the string. If the tuner leaves the tension different on the two ends of the string that you cannot hear, the tension will gradually equalize over a few minutes or hours and put the piano slightly out of tune again. For a tuner to tune stably takes an enormous amount of skill. To tune as stably as Barry did is extremely unusual.

There was another reason why Barry hated sitting there all day at the recording studio. It was especially boring for him, because he was completely blind, and there was nothing there for him to do. He couldn't see a light shined directly into his eyes, since he had been injured in a car accident when he was nine years old. Barry told me that rather than feeling sorry for himself, he decided to treat life as if it were a game and he were wearing a blindfold. He was fun and upbeat. I found him to be a great inspiration for bringing a positive outlook to life.

Barry was happily married to a very sweet and beautiful woman who would occasionally sneak into the piano shop and come up behind him and put her hands over his eyes like the game "Guess Who?" He would say, "Now who could that be? Let me see!" It was funny and delightful to watch every time they did it. They had a wonderful affection for each other.

Barry sang in a quartet of African-American blind young men. They were hoping to make a career of their music, and they sang well-known songs, known as "standards," beautifully in close harmony. Their sighted manager drove them to gigs in a yellow Cadillac. The piano shop where we worked was their rehearsal space. After rehearsal, I'd see them out walking on the street, laughing and relaxed as if they could see. None of them bothered to use their white canes, because the sound of their banter acted as "shadow vision." They could hear the sound bouncing off the buildings, so they could determine where they were. It was amazing to watch. You would swear they could see, but none of them could. Barry was the lead singer in the group. The warmth, smoothness, and beauty of his voice were remarkable.

He also sang when we had holiday parties at the piano store. We would get a small group of musicians together to perform. Harold, another blind tuner who worked at the store, would play the accompaniment for songs on the piano. Bart, a sighted tuner, would play the harmonica, and Barry would sing. When he would sing songs like

Misty, or *Smoke Gets in Your Eyes,* the women office workers would sigh. It was a happy time.

I learned a lot from Barry about getting around in the world. The piano store had an old back building that had dozens of priceless art-carved Steinway pianos on three floors, and sometimes we had to go back there for parts or supplies. This was not a modern building. It was made around the turn of the last century and the freight elevators were scary. Barry would take me up in the freight elevator in the dark to the lightless warehouse and walk around in front of me until we found the lights. Barry confronted that darkness every hour of every day. He was a courageous person. I learned to have my fears and to go ahead in life without the fears stopping me as much. It was a valuable lesson for me.

Barry was a very special person, an amazing piano tuner, and someone whom I'll always appreciate and remember. In life, we all have challenges that seem overwhelming at the time. It has always helped me to face my difficulties, by remembering the grace and courage with which Barry faced his.

Steinert Hall – A Lost Boston Landmark

THE STEINWAY FRANCHISE OF BOSTON WAS named M. Steinert and Sons. The store was in a six-story building which was constructed in 1896, and located at 162 Boylston Street across from Boston Common. When I worked there in 1972, only a few people knew that 35' underground, beneath the main building was a concert hall, known as Steinert Hall. It was the elite small concert hall of Boston from 1896 – 1942, seating only 650 people.

The Steinert building was six stories high above ground and had pumps on the roof that transferred fresh air from the roof and released it through holes in the floor of the subterranean concert hall. The hall was luxuriously furnished with ornate plasterwork, frescoes, columns, and large plaques displaying the names of famous composers around the hall. The entrance for patrons was through a grand staircase that led down from the building entrance, which was at street level. Concert pianos were brought down to the concert hall on a large freight elevator. There are still records of famous musicians having performed there to elite audiences.

The concert hall was closed in 1942 after the city fire regulations were changed to require more than one exit on all public buildings. Steinert Hall had only a single exit. Since it was underground and built out to the edge of the property in every dimension, there was no way that additional exits could be constructed. Because the hall could not meet the new fire regulation standards, it was closed to the public. As a result, it was largely forgotten and became a lost landmark of Boston.

When I was a new employee at Steinert's, one of the veteran employees, Bart, told me about the hall, and offered to take me on a tour. There were no windows and no lighting, so we each had to take a flashlight. We slipped single file down a narrow back staircase that looked like it had not been used in decades. The paint was falling off the walls in large patches. The staircase wound down four floors from our second floor shop. At one point we passed large coal-fired boilers that must have originally supplied the heat for the building, but Bart thought that the building originally produced its own electricity, as well. It was getting pretty spooky by this point, with just the flashlights for illumination, and darkness all around us wherever the lights were not pointed. It occurred to me that no one knew we were down there, in case something happened.

Finally, a great expanse opened in front of us, and it was the concert hall. Although it was a state-of-the-art concert hall when it was built, it had really deteriorated over the years due to water damage and neglect. Paint was falling off the walls and there was water on the floor. The audience seating had been removed and old storage crates and junk were scattered across the hall. I noticed one large wooden crate that had been designed to hold a 9' concert grand piano for transport by train. It had large lettering on the side advertising the brand of the piano and the performing artist's name. The whole place looked more like a movie set than anything I had ever seen in real life. It was an intense experience for me, seeing such an unusual place.

Steinert Hall was always fascinating to me, so years later I did a search on the internet and found a great deal of information. If you do a search for Steinert Hall, you will find a video tour on Youtube. Compared to my visit there, the hall does not look nearly as eerie on the video, since they had lighting at the time of the filming. You can get some of the feel for the faded ornate beauty of the place, though. Your search may also find a lot of still pictures of the hall, and an article from 2015 announcing that the building was sold to a developer who plans to restore the hall and have concerts there again. No mention was made about the problem of having enough fire exits. The hall is in an elliptical shape, which gives great acoustics, and it is 35' underground, which eliminates any extraneous sound disturbing the music. If you are ever in Boston after the restoration is complete, it would certainly be worthwhile to attend a concert there.

THE STORY OF GLADYS TROUPIN AND GEORGE GERSHWIN

G LADYS TROUPIN WAS AN ICON OF BOSTON'S cultural life during the 1960's and 70's. From 1964-1978, she played piano in Diamond Jim's, an upscale bar in the lobby of the Lenox Hotel. Diamond Jim's was a popular spot for Boston nightlife. Performers from touring musicals would often stop by the bar after performances, and they would sing a few songs accompanied by Gladys. Patrons could hang out at the bar and often hear famous performers.

Gladys was born in 1898, so she was ages 66-80 during that time that she played nightly at Diamond Jim's. She was known and respected for several things. Musically, she could play almost any song in any key. Her ability to play in any key was particularly endearing to singers, because this allowed them to show off their voices to their best advantage. For example, if a singer was not feeling their best, Gladys could lower the key a half-tone, so the singer would not need to strain for the high notes.

She always wore elegant dresses and spectacular hats,

so that she looked like someone who had walked right out of the 1890's. Her curly white hair contrasted beautifully with her colorful attire. One of her most striking outfits included a matching apricot dress and hat. She was a pleasing sight all on her own, even though her main ability and rare gift was to help show off the voices of singers.

Another aspect of Gladys' fame was that she was believed to have been engaged to George Gershwin. During the 1970's, whenever Gladys' name was brought up within Boston music circles, it was common for someone to say, "You know, she was engaged to George Gershwin at the time of his death."

During the mid-seventies, I was hired to tune Gladys' performance piano at the Lenox Hotel. I would tune the Steinway piano at the hotel once a week in the daytime, but Gladys would arrive to perform in the evening. As a result, although I had tuned the piano numerous times, I had never met her. Then, one day I unexpectedly received a call directly from Gladys asking me to tune her home piano.

She lived in an apartment in a high-rise at the Prudential Center in Boston, which was within walking distance of the Lenox Hotel. It was a pleasure to meet her, and after I finished tuning her piano, she wanted to chat a bit with me. We talked about many things. I was able to ask her how she learned so many songs and how she developed the ability to transpose music to different keys. She explained that she spent her career teaching musical comedy at a nearby college. When I commented that she must really love to perform, since she was out playing every night at her age, she said, "Are you kidding? I do it because it pays the rent!"

She also was willing to talk about George Gershwin. Gladys told me the following account:

Porgy and Bess was first performed at the Colonial Theater in Boston on September 30, 1935, before it opened in New York. Gladys took her son to the opening performance and they were able to meet Gershwin backstage after the show. According to Gladys, she and Gershwin had an immediate mutual attraction and he had a fondness for her son, as well. She said that Gershwin always had a very hectic schedule, but that he and Gladys were able to see each other fairly frequently and they were eventually engaged. She also told me the shocking way that she found out about the death of Gershwin. When she was leaving Boston to travel to San Francisco for the opening of *Porgy and Bess* there, she walked by a newsstand and saw the headlines, "Gershwin Dead at 39!"

I always cherished that first hand story from Gladys about one of our nation's greatest composers. Recently, though, I read that Gershwin had lived in Beverly Hills during the last few years of his life, and that he had been dating various movie stars during that time. Since this conflicted with the story Gladys told me, I decided to investigate it further.

I started out by checking on the internet. I found out that Gershwin and Gladys Troupin were both born in 1898, and that Gershwin died before his birthday in 1937 at the age of 38, not 39, as Gladys had said. You might wonder how I am so sure she said 39, and not 38. I remember this because of the horrible *faux pas* I made in the conversation that followed. After she told me about the newspaper headline, she said, "It's amazing how many great musicians have died at age 39." Without thinking of how insensitive it was of me, I blurted out, "Yes. My favorite was Jack Benny." Of course, she didn't find it amusing.

Because of the discrepancies between the story Gladys told me and the information I had read about Gershwin in Hollywood, I decided to investigate it even further. I looked for a biography of Gershwin to see if I could find a definitive answer about their engagement. I discovered there were several biographies available, and I chose the one by Rodney Greenberg, which I found to be extremely interesting and easy to read.

Gershwin's private life was well documented in Greenberg's book, but there was no mention of Gladys Troupin, nor was there mention of any trips to Boston during the last two years of his life. According to Greenberg, Gershwin was never engaged, and just before his death he wrote a note to Kay Swift, with whom he had had his longest relationship, asking if they could get back together.

Evidently, one of the recurrent themes of Gershwin's life was his inability to have a successful relationship with a woman. It was said that he frequently complained to others that he didn't understand why his friends and relatives had great marriages and relationships, yet he could not manage it. Greenberg quotes Oscar Levant, a close friend of Gershwin's, as quipping, "There goes Mr. George Gershwin and the future Miss Kay Swift."

Although it certainly appears that it was not a true story about the engagement, it was still a delightful tale that many people heard and loved to retell. Some people might object at having been fooled by her, but I don't think Gladys meant any harm. I think she gave us all something special in our lives. Also, you never know. Gershwin could have had a secret second life, and maybe he really was engaged to her. There's no knowing for sure, but it seems unlikely. Regardless, it's all fun and very colorful, and I am happy that I had a chance to know such a delightful, interesting, and talented person.

Meeting Gladys gave me an additional gift, because it inspired me to read the biography of Gershwin. Greenberg's writing really brought Gershwin alive to me, and it allowed me to appreciate the struggles of a real person, rather than just the image of a musical icon. Like many people, I assumed that Gershwin enjoyed fame and success his entire life. In reality, he had many set-backs, and he endured relentless criticism from the music critics of his day.

For example, contrary to what Gladys related, there was not a planned opening of *Porgy and Bess* in San Francisco in 1937. Sadly, *Porgy and Bess* closed in New York after only 124 performances. Trying to recoup some of their losses, the Gershwins took the opera on tour, but only to Philadelphia, Pittsburgh, Chicago, and Washington, D.C., and that tour ended a year before Gershwin died. The first west coast production was the year after Gershwin's death. The opera was widely appreciated only after revivals in the 1950's and 1980's. It is now accepted as the premier twentieth century opera, but during Gershwin's lifetime it was not widely acclaimed. Greenberg reports that Gershwin received only $10,000 in royalties from the production, and that amount did not even cover his copying expenses. He and his brother, Ira, had financed the production and they lost a great deal of money on it.

Finding out more about Gershwin's life, I have gained a lot more perspective on several seemingly unrelated events that I had encountered before. For example, one of my favorite songs is "Love is Here to Stay." I often play it on customers' pianos after I've tuned them. I learned that it was the last song Gershwin wrote, and that he did not finish it. His brother Ira Gershwin and Oscar Levant finished it. It was first used in a forgettable movie called the *Goldwyn Follies*, produced by Sam Goldwyn, the "G" in MGM. Goldwyn had insulted the Gershwin brothers, requiring them to audition the songs for him for the movie, and docking George a day's pay whenever he was unable to work because of his brain cancer. After all that, *Goldwyn Follies* was a useless movie that closed immediately and all of the songs were buried for 15 years. "Love is Here to Stay" became well-known only after Gene Kelly sang it to his French girlfriend in the movie, *An American in Paris* in 1951.

Another interesting connection for me from the biography, was Greenberg's description of Serge Koussevitsky's reaction to Gershwin's piano playing. Koussevitsky was the music director of the Boston Symphony Orchestra in the 1930's, and he is legendary in Boston. Koussevitsky also founded Tanglewood, a music venue in the Berkshire Hills area of western Massachusetts. Tanglewood is the summer home of the Boston Symphony, and it is also home to three music schools for gifted young musicians.

Koussevitsky had worked with the greatest musicians of his day, yet when he heard Gershwin improvise at the piano, he remarked that he wondered if he were imagining it, as Gershwin's playing seemed too extraordinary to be real.

MEETING AARON COPLAND

IN THE 1970'S, THE BOSTON SYMPHONY Orchestra changed their method of arranging for choruses to sing with the orchestra. Prior to 1970, they would hire a local chorus such as the Chorus Pro Musica or the Handel and Hayden Society to perform with the orchestra. Those choruses consisted of amateurs, so a $1,000 payment to the chorus was sufficient for the amateur singers to jump at the opportunity of singing with the orchestra.

The change of policy that the symphony chose was to create their own dedicated chorus to sing in performances with the orchestra. They named the chorus the Tanglewood Festival Chorus, after the summer home of the orchestra, which is located in western Massachusetts. The Tanglewood Chorus would sing with the orchestra several weekends in the winter season at Symphony Hall in Boston, and then the chorus would sing at Tanglewood three or four weekends during July and August.

In the fall of 1974, I auditioned for the chorus and I was accepted. In the winter season we would rehearse one night a week for our performances at Symphony Hall. For the three or four weekends that we would perform in the summer, we would provide our own transportation out to the Berkshire Mountains in western Massachusetts on Wednesdays. For our accommodations, the orchestra rented a dormitory at a private residential high school nearby. Rehearsals were during the day on Thursday and Friday, and the performances were on Friday night, Saturday night, and/or Sunday afternoon.

The Friday night concerts drew smaller crowds and the concerts were often a mix of smaller pieces of music, whereas the Saturday and Sunday concerts usually featured a major symphony or other well-known piece of music to draw the crowds. All the concerts were at the "Shed," a covered structure that was open to the air on three sides. The Shed seemed a perfect design for the venue, in that you felt the outdoor air, but were protected from the rain and sun.

One Friday night, those of us in the Tanglewood Chorus were seated on stage for a choral number, waiting while another piece of music was performed just before ours. It was Aaron Copland's *Quiet City* directed by Copland himself. I had never seen him before and I was unfamiliar with *Quiet City*. It is a piece for solo trumpet with orchestral accompaniment. To me, it seemed to be written as if a street musician were playing a trumpet on a city street late in the night, except of course, it was virtuoso playing of astoundingly beautiful music. Listening to it being played outdoors at night and directed by Copland himself, was pure magic.

The chorus was seated behind the orchestra, and I was seated in the center of the first row of the chorus, so I had a great vantage point, being only about 30 feet directly in front of Mr. Copland, and only a few feet behind and to the side of the solo trumpet player. It was mesmerizing. I don't have the slightest memory of our choral performance that followed, or even what piece of music we performed. All I remember is the wistful sound of that trumpet in the pure night mountain air.

The next day, several of us were sitting on the lawn behind the Shed. We were there to listen to the open rehearsal. Each Saturday morning, the symphony would rehearse the programs for the Saturday night and Sunday afternoon performances. These were known as "open rehearsals" since music students could sit down close to the orchestra and listen and learn as the conductor worked with the orchestra to get the performance he envisioned. It was always very interesting and educational. The Shed was located on a hill with a large lawn at the back. Prior to performances, many patrons would bring blankets, food, and candelabras and have dinner or lunch on the lawn and listen to the concerts afterwards. It was a lot like a post-card setting. From the lawn, you could see the lake down below, surrounded by woods. It was very peaceful and beautiful.

During the open rehearsal that day, my friends and I were relaxing on the lawn listening to the music and enjoying the view of the lake. We noticed an unusual-looking group of people maybe thirty yards away who were talking together and walking toward us. One fellow had a big black beard and wore a large white robe. He had a red headband and a large head of curly black hair. One of my friends said, "Look at that guy. He looks just like a guru." There were a few others with very distinctive outfits as well. Then one of my friends pointed out a tall thin older gentleman, kind of hunched forward a little bit, with a large prominent nose. I was thinking, "Ichabod Crane," but one of my friends said, "Look at that guy! He looks just like a composer." We all had a good laugh.

Then as they got closer, we gasped as we realized the person who looked like a composer really *was* a composer. It was Aaron Copland with his retinue. Somebody in our group said, "Oh my gosh, he really *is* a composer!" Something about the situation was so unexpected that it caught us all off guard and we started laughing hysterically and rolling around on the lawn, saying, "He is a composer!"

We were all so absorbed in the humor of the situation that we didn't notice Aaron Copland had arrived at our gathering. He looked down at me and asked, "What's so funny?"

I looked up at him and said, "Uh, uh..." and I couldn't even talk. For one thing, I was afraid that he might think we were making fun of him, as opposed to just laughing at the completely unexpected occurrence. On top of that, I felt frightened to talk to someone who was so famous. Finally, I managed to say, "The *Quiet City* last night was wonderful."

He replied, "Oh, thanks," and then he turned and walked on. He wasn't interested in being admired; he just wanted to visit with us, but I was too tongue-tied to do so. In my defense, none of my friends were able to utter a word, either. It's a shame that I did not know more about Copland at the time, or I might have been able to have a conversation with him.

I read later that Copland had spent a lot of his adult life encouraging young musicians to develop and pursue their musical talents. Prior to the time we met him, he had taught composition at Tanglewood for ten years. He loved encouraging and inspiring young composers, never forgetting how difficult and challenging his own early years were as a musician.

When he was growing up in Brooklyn, Copland was the youngest child in a large family. His parents had obtained music lessons for some of his older siblings, but none of them had shown much interest or talent. By the time Aaron came along, his parents didn't think it was worth the investment, so they refused his repeated requests for lessons. Finally, he resorted to paying his older sister for his piano lessons. He learned so quickly that he was soon able to audition and be accepted into a music school. Over the years of his study in various schools, his main interest turned to composition, but his teachers repeatedly told him that his music was too unusual and unrestrained. Finally, he was sent to a woman composition teacher, Nadia Boulanger. At the time, no one believed that a woman could teach composition anyway, so people thought the two of them would be a good match. They were. She was the first to give him encouragement to write the unique music that he imagined.

If I had known all this at the time, I might have appreciated that he simply enjoyed visiting with young musicians, and I may have been able to hold up my end of a conversation with him. I have often regretted that I missed an opportunity to talk with America's premier living composer. While that is true, I realize that fame was not the most important characteristic of Mr. Copland. More importantly, he was a great role model of a person who pursued the expression of his own musical vision even in the face of almost universal criticism from the authorities of his day. Additionally, he was someone

41

who never forgot how difficult his early years were, and who contributed much of his time and energy to helping young musicians.

Writing memoirs, as I am doing now, is an interesting endeavor. When writing, the temptation is to modify the memories to fit a rational scheme, so that it all makes sense. Although I still cannot make any sense of my inability to carry on a conversation with Aaron Copland, I am very happy that I at least had a very brief encounter with him on that day.

Perhaps the value I can derive is that the memory of a conversation did not end up overshadowing my memory of the experience of his music. Whenever I wish, I can still hear that trumpet playing in the night mountain air, and it is a wonderful memory.

CHRISTMAS AT POPS WITH ARTHUR FIEDLER

MANY PEOPLE BELIEVE THAT ARTHUR Fiedler founded the Boston Pops Orchestra (POPS). In fact, the POPS was founded in 1885 by Henry Lee Higginson, who had founded the Boston Symphony Orchestra (BSO) just four years earlier in 1881. The Boston Pops Orchestra typically uses many of the same instrumentalists that play in the BSO. It's mission is to play a lighter fare of music that would be more popular for a wider audience than those who attend the BSO concerts.

The likely reason that people often believe that Fiedler founded the POPS, is that he was their director for 49 years. Prior to his taking the baton in 1930, there had been 17 conductors in the first 45 years of the orchestra's existence. Fiedler ended up being conductor of the POPS longer than all of the previous 17 conductors combined. In fact, by the 1970's, most people could not even recall the POPS ever having had any other conductor.

It was Fiedler who instituted the free outdoor concerts on the esplanade next to the Charles River. He also started the *Evening at Pops* television shows on public television, and he was the first to make a recording of the complete *Rhapsody in Blue* of George Gershwin.

Another of his creations was a brilliant program of Christmas music, called *Christmas at Pops with Arthur Fiedler*. Three performances were scheduled over a single weekend in December. There was one show on Saturday afternoon, a second one on Saturday night, and then a third one on Sunday afternoon. All the performances were at Symphony Hall in Boston, and all of them were led by Fiedler. In the winter of 1974, WGBH, the public TV channel for Boston, filmed the Saturday afternoon performance, and it aired on public television stations nationwide for years afterward.

The Tanglewood Chorus performed all the choral numbers in the program, and I was fortunate enough to have joined the chorus that year. Our regular choral director led our rehearsals, accompanied by piano, for a few weeks prior to rehearsing with Fiedler and the orchestra. Our choral conductor joked that this music was "tinsel" compared with the weighty pieces we usually sang with the BSO. Most of the Christmas choral pieces were commercial adaptations of traditional music, so it was pretty showy stuff.

The week before the performance we had our first rehearsal with the orchestra led by Arthur Fiedler. I was expecting Mr. Fiedler to be a jovial, humorous character similar to what I had seen on TV. Boy, was I wrong. He was all business. I was surprised at the time, until it hit me that this was how he consistently had such excellent results. He was not at all into joking around with the instrumentalists. Instead, he was completely focused on work from the very first minute down to the last minute of rehearsal time in order to produce the best music he possibly could.

You may not know that most orchestra musicians are union members. Their contracts stipulate how much time can be spent in a rehearsal before they start getting overtime. There is a large clock prominently displayed during rehearsal, and conductors will start to the minute on time and end exactly to the minute as well. It works extremely well. In contrast, I have occasionally seen amateurish choral conductors abuse the good nature of their amateur singers by over-rehearsing, so I can imagine what it could have been like in orchestra rehearsals before unions were formed.

Fiedler always saved the jovial part for the live performances, so Christmas performances with him were a lot of fun. The audience could join in and sing along with many of the Christmas songs. The afternoon performance was packed with little girls dressed in their best dresses and young boys with coats and ties. At one point in the show Santa would make an entrance through the audience up to the stage to present Fiedler with a red Santa hat of his own. Fiedler had a white beard, so he looked just like Santa when he put his red hat on.

I actually enjoyed the instrumental pieces that were played even more than the choral pieces. The orchestra played Leroy Anderson's highly popular *Sleigh Ride,* which I had often heard on recordings of the POPS. I remember being directly behind the trumpet player when he made the sound of a whinnying horse at the very end. *Sleigh Ride* was a signature piece of music for the orchestra.

Christmas at Pops had an exhausting performance schedule for all of us. Never before or since have I been part of three performances in two days. We barely had time to grab a bite to eat between performances on Saturday. It takes a great deal of energy to sing for long hours, and we were completely wiped out by the end. The Christmas rush is always the busiest time of the year for a piano tuner, so it took a lot of energy to juggle all the rehearsals and performances in addition to the extra tunings I was doing for clients' Christmas parties and concerts. That December, I was also performing three concerts with the Chorus Pro Musica. Those concerts also had rehearsals and parties, as well. It was a wild ride and yet ridiculously fun, to celebrate Christmas in Boston.

One of the best perks of doing these POPS performances was that my family and I could watch the film on TV each Christmas for several years. It was probably expensive to film the show, so the public television network just replayed the same tape each year. I know it must have been a lot of fun for my parents to see, and I'll always appreciate the incredible experience.

THE AMERICAN BICENTENNIAL CELEBRATION

A S I PREVIOUSLY MENTIONED, THE PEOPLE of Boston have a unique pride and affection for the Boston Symphony Orchestra (BSO). I had an opportunity to experience that appreciation first hand in an unexpected way in 1976, the year we celebrated our nation's bicentennial. During the course of that entire year there were events scheduled all over Boston, but there was one that was particularly memorable for me. It was a summer outdoor concert by the BSO and the Tanglewood Festival Chorus held at the Boston Common, a huge park in downtown Boston.

I had been a member of the Tanglewood Chorus for a couple years at that point. It was unusual for us to perform in Boston in the summer. We normally performed in Boston only in the winter, and at Tanglewood in western Massachusetts in the summer. The summer weekends were paradise. In the mornings, we would go to rehearsals with Seiji Ozawa or some other famous conductor, such as Carlo Maria Giulini or Andre Previn. We would have time to go down to the lake and swim with friends in the afternoons. With 119 friends, you could always find someone to have fun with. At concerts, we would dress up in our white dinner jackets for the men and white dresses for the women and sing the most beautiful music ever written with some of the finest musicians in the world. We were not paid, but all our expenses were taken care of. As amateurs, we couldn't have been happier.

For the concert at the Boston Common in 1976, we all wore our white concert attire and met at Symphony Hall about a mile from Boston Common. After a quick warm-up, we were directed to board several buses outside the hall. The buses had large signs on the sides that proclaimed *Boston Symphony Orchestra*. There were 120 members of the chorus and about 100 members of the orchestra with their instruments, so it required a few buses to manage transporting all of us. As a result, it took quite a while for all of us to climb in and find our seats. We expected to have further delays, too, with a slow ride through clogged city streets to the Common.

Once we were ready to depart, we were startled by multiple police sirens as the buses took off like drag racers. We didn't know that the city had prepared a motorcycle escort, nor that they had closed off Boylston Street all along the route to the Common. It felt like we were driving 60 miles an hour, but it probably was only 40 miles an hour down this major thoroughfare with at least a dozen police motorcycles around us with their sirens screaming. The street was densely lined with people as if they had come for a parade. The signs on the side of the buses proclaimed who we were. The crowds were cheering and whistling and waving at us as we roared by. It was astounding. We were screaming with delight like first graders. I've never experienced anything like it. It was the kind of reception cities give to returning baseball world champions. I guess Boston hadn't had one of those for about 60 years at that point, so maybe that contributed to their appreciation and enthusiasm for their orchestra, which they all knew was one of the world's best. It seemed like the whole city had turned out to line the route and crowd the Common. We arrived at the Common to huge crowds of people cheering. Man, it was fun to feel like a celebrity for a few minutes. I can't remember a bit of the concert we sang, but I'll never forget that ride and the great display of pride and appreciation from the people of Boston for their orchestra.

Mom Sings at Tanglewood

M Y MOTHER, WINNIE KLEIN, HAD A GREAT gift, or you could say two great gifts. Not only did she have a remarkable voice, she also understood how to use it to express beauty. A fair amount of people have excellent voices which are dramatic and impressive, but it is unusual to find someone who can express great beauty with their voice. Music teachers tell me that expressing beauty through music cannot be taught, but rather it is an expression of one's inner spiritual and emotional make-up. When I was a child, people would often stop my mother in the supermarket or after church to tell her how moved they were by her singing. In our community she was widely admired, yet she handled it with quiet dignity rather than with any conceit.

Mom was a high soprano, but she also had a three-octave range that was even and smooth top to bottom. Sundays, and especially on holidays, she would be the soloist at church. Also, for many years in the springtime she would be the lead on stage at the local community theater's Gilbert and Sullivan operetta. Mom could sing an E above high C, which is required for the lead in *Pirates of Penzance*. Not many sopranos have that high of a range, so she was a shoo-in for the role.

She was always a role model for me in her commitment to her music and to her personal expression through it. Even though she was an amateur, she practiced daily and took her performance preparation very seriously. She had begun performing in New York in the 1930's. During much of the depression, married women were not allowed to hold jobs, so she would practice her piano playing and singing for several hours a day. She studied voice with a well-known teacher, Margaret Bristol. Ms. Bristol promoted her studio by placing her students in a women's chorus that performed on radio programs with my mother as the soloist. Our family has saved some of the old 78 rpm recordings of those performances. One of them included the announcer before the performance saying, "And now, Winnie Klein and the Girls Ensemble will sing 'Safire Seas'."

My parents arranged for me to study several instruments, including voice. All those lessons have been of immense value to me as an adult, and I am very grateful that my parents provided them. As an adult, I took the opportunity to thank them for requiring me to practice daily as a child, even though my piano practice was often done tearfully and against my will.

When I was accepted into the Tanglewood Chorus, I invited my parents to drive up to Tanglewood from Delaware to hear a performance. They happily agreed to make the trip. In preparation for their visit, I learned the piano accompaniment for one of my mother's favorite duets, "Bess, You is My Woman Now," from *Porgy and Bess*.

I'm not a great pianist, so I had to practice for a couple months before I could sing the baritone part and play the piano at the same time.

While they were visiting at Tanglewood, my parents had the opportunity to attend our rehearsals, as well as the performances. Mom loved the opportunity to be in such an all-encompassing musical environment. One day during a break between rehearsals, my girlfriend, my parents, and I went for a walk around the grounds. At one point we stood in the side doorway of one of the barns, where the Berkshire Orchestra was rehearsing. In addition to being the summer home of the Boston Symphony Orchestra, Tanglewood has instruction for gifted young performers from all over the world. Young people can study their instruments with world renown artists, and they get opportunities to perform as soloists, in small ensembles, in the Berkshire Chorus, and in the Berkshire Orchestra. Rehearsals at Tanglewood are held in buildings called "barns." I believe they really were barns in an earlier era, when the property was a farm. They were very clean and well-maintained, but the structures were certainly those of barns. You could see the wooden beams holding up two-story-high roofs. There was no interior wallboard nor separate rooms to make it look like a finished building. Our side door position allowed us an unobstructed view of the conductor in profile. We watched the Berkshire Orchestra for a few moments before my girl friend whispered the name of the conductor to us. It was Leonard Bernstein! We were all pretty excited, as none of us had ever seen him before. It seemed like a dream to be there watching him work with the young musicians.

After the rehearsal, the barn emptied and we stayed

for a little while talking. I had the sheet music with me for the duet, and I asked my mom if she wanted to sing it with me. She was a little reluctant, and looked around to see if anyone would object. We were the only ones there, so she agreed. It seemed like the rehearsal piano was sitting there waiting for us. I put the music on the music desk, and together we sang, "Bess You Is My Woman Now." For a barn, the building was quite resonant, so it sounded pretty good. My mother's voice was very clear and carried well, so it was very beautiful. There is something very special about family members playing music and singing together, and it is one of my favorite Tanglewood memories.

STRAVINSKY'S
OEDIPUS REX

STRAVINSKY'S *OEDIPUS REX* WAS A GROUND-breaking opera-oratorio that is considered by some scholars to be the best example of Stravinsky's neoclassical period. It premiered in France in 1927, and the American premier was presented by the Boston Symphony Orchestra (BSO) in 1928. In 1981, the Boston Symphony announced that this work would be performed by the orchestra with the Tanglewood Chorus the following year. Because of its complexity, Stravinsky's *Oedipus Rex* is rarely performed, so its upcoming concert was widely anticipated.

Originally, the 1982 production with the BSO was scheduled for three performances in February at Symphony Hall in Boston, and a single performance the following weekend at Carnegie Hall in New York. The Tanglewood Chorus began rehearsals of the music in the previous autumn. The work would require a lot of preparation, as the chorus score was ninety pages of difficult modern music with Latin lyrics. Additionally, it was all to be memorized, as we would be in costume performing movements and dance steps, as well. A prominent professional stage director was brought in to teach us the movements that we would be performing on stage. It was to be staged like a Greek tragedy, and we were the Greek chorus, reacting to the various events of the story. The six soloists also sang in Latin, so Stravinsky scored a narrator in order to help the audience keep track of the plot. Originally, the narration was written in French, but an English translation would be used for our production.

After a few weeks of chorus rehearsals, the narrator was announced. It was to be Vanessa Redgrave. That is when the wheels began falling off. She had previously given an interview expressing her support for the Palestinian Liberation Organization (PLO), and many of the financial backers of the orchestra were extremely opposed to the PLO. The fear of withdrawal of financial backing was very unsettling to the symphony management, so it was no surprise that after a few weeks of negotiations, Ms. Redgrave was replaced.

Many perceived this as censorship, since an artist was fired for expressing a particular political belief, and it created a backlash. The stage director, choreographer, and other contract personnel felt it was important for them to leave the production as well, so as not to condone that type of suppression of personal expression.

Without these people, the scheduled concert could not go on. For example, we could not use the stage direction we had been taught, since it was all the work of the exiting stage director. At this point, there was not enough time for a new stage director to come in and teach us entirely new movements. An additional complication was that we were also scheduled to take the show to Carnegie Hall in

New York after the production in Boston. Therefore, the concert in New York had to be changed as well.

Oedipus Rex was quickly replaced with the Berlioz *Requiem*. It requires a brass choir in a balcony at the back of the hall, so it is somewhat dramatic. It would not be as spectacular a show as *Oedipus Rex*, but it was the best that we could do with only a few weeks of preparation.

I was fortunate to have performed the Berlioz previously with the Chorus Pro Musica, so it was not very difficult for me to prepare the music quickly. Most other members of the chorus, however, needed to put in a lot of extra hours in order to learn the music in time for the performance. Additionally, after the Carnegie Hall concert, we were scheduled to perform Beethoven's *Ninth Symphony* the following night at Lincoln Center, so all of the singers who were not familiar with that work had double the preparation.

The performances of the Berlioz in Boston went very well, and the following week we all went to New York. Most of us had never sung in either Carnegie Hall or Lincoln Center, so we were very excited. Carnegie Hall is slightly larger than Symphony Hall in Boston, and it is very ornate and beautiful. It has an enormously high ceiling, allowing seating on five levels. The color scheme of gold and white makes it feel like a piece of jewelry.

The rehearsal at Carnegie Hall was particularly fun. There are three balconies at the back of the hall. Seiji Ozawa, the director of the orchestra, wanted to hear the brass choir a couple times from each balcony, so that he could decide which sounded the best. He was clearly enjoying himself during rehearsal as he would turn and yell to the back of the hall, "One more time, from the balcony above (or below)." Then the whole brass choir would tromp up or down a flight or two of stairs and set up their music stands and we would all play that section again. None of us minded, though, because it was the most exciting section of the music. I can still recall that the rehearsal number of that section was "33." We all smiled each time at the joy in Ozawa's voice as he would start again by saying, "One more time! Thirty-three!"

The performances of the Berlioz and the Beethoven went well, and the tour was considered a success.

A few weeks after those performances, the Boston Symphony management announced that *Oedipus Rex* would be performed at Tanglewood the following summer. Once again, we began our weekly rehearsals in Boston. We were able to keep our usual rehearsal choral conductor, but the stage director and choreographer were replaced. This meant that we would need to learn new movements, as well as new dance steps.

Sam Wanamaker was hired as the new stage director, and he was a delight to work with. He was warm and compassionate, and his ideas made a lot of sense. He had us do sweeping grand movements, which would be clearly visible in a large hall. Wanamaker issued each of us a two-foot square piece of thick cape-like cloth that was black on one side and white on the other. We were to display and/or wave these in synchrony with the mood of the narrative and in time with the music. White fabric would be displayed during happy sequences, and dark fabric during the tragic scenes.

The new choreographer was from a premier contemporary dance troupe, so she was used to working with professional dancers. Not only were we amateurs, but most of the chorus had never had any type of instruction in dance or movement. At times the choreographer seemed barely able to contain her frustration while working with us.

None of us had ever experienced a performance that had more mishaps. For example, the headliner soprano lost her voice and had to be replaced at the last minute. The tenor soloist fell off a riser, hit his head knocking him unconscious, and had to be rushed to the hospital. In the middle of all this was a chorus of 100 people who were accustomed to performing only while standing in one place and reading their music. For this performance, though, we had memorized 90 pages of modern music with lyrics in Latin. We were dressed in costume and while singing, we were performing dance steps and at the same time waving the correct color of cloth in unison. There was no room for error.

All of this elaborate preparation was for a single performance on a Saturday night at Tanglewood. Fortunately, it came off spectacularly well. Seiji Ozawa, the conductor, was not the least bit perturbed by any of the mishaps that we had along the way. He never wavered in his commitment to the power and drama of the work. He held all of the disparate parts together into a superlative performance, and his musical interpretation was pure genius. The experience of that music was unlike any I have ever had. The chord progressions and rhythm changes were such that it stimulated a new realm of emotional experience in the listener. In the middle of the performance, I was astounded at how powerful an effect the music had on me.

The audience jumped up and cheered wildly for numerous curtain calls at the end. I had never seen an audience at Tanglewood respond so enthusiastically about a performance. A lot of people had traveled long distances to see *Oedipus Rex* that night, since the performances in New York and Boston had been cancelled. It was a memorable night, and well worth all of the trouble and effort.

Seiji Ozawa

SEIJI OZAWA WAS HONORED IN 2015 AT THE Kennedy Center in Washington, D.C. for a lifetime of contributions to American musical culture. The ceremony was shown on public TV, detailing over fifty years that he conducted the world's major orchestras and opera companies. Ozawa was one of the more fascinating characters I ever encountered. He was the music director of the Boston Symphony in the 1970's and 80's, when I sang in the Tanglewood Chorus. As if directing the Boston Symphony wasn't enough to keep him busy, he was also music director of the San Francisco Symphony at the same time. He directed most of the performances that the Tanglewood Chorus had with the Boston Symphony, so I got to perform with him frequently. At the times when he was out of town, our performances would be directed by other famous guest conductors from around the world, so the chorus got to compare how they all conducted. Ozawa was by far the most interesting and enjoyable to perform with.

Ozawa was qualitatively different from other conductors in a few ways. One was his aesthetic movement. He was not just beating time and gesturing with his hands, like other conductors. He would use his entire body to convey the expression of the music that he was directing. It was as if he were dancing in place without moving his feet. Another way to say it would be that he was like a supple tree swaying in a strong wind. Audiences loved to watch him direct, since he added a visual dimension to his interpretation of the music. A second quality he exhibited was his intensity. Whether slow or fast, loud or soft, the intensity of his presence held everyone tightly to his direction, so that the music that was produced had a magical quality. When he took the podium, he would stand with his hands crossed in front of him and close his eyes for a few seconds. Then he would open his eyes with a fervor that grabbed every player's attention. There was never a moment that anyone's attention wavered during an entire performance. As a result of his intensity, every performance was of extraordinary quality. The third characteristic was his memory. He would show up at the first rehearsal of every piece with the entire score memorized. No other conductor did that. Even for the Schoenberg *Gurre-Lieder,* one of the largest and least performed works, he had the entire score memorized, all for a single performance at Tanglewood. During rehearsals an assistant would be seated next to the podium. The assistant would follow along in the score as the rehearsal progressed. If Ozawa wanted to stop for a correction and restart from a specific place, the assistant would then announce which rehearsal number in the score for all of us to restart together from the same place.

For example, there was one memorable rehearsal where we had a restart. The *Gurre-Lieder* has three men's choruses, plus a mixed chorus for spectacular volume in some for the segments. The men's choruses were intended to be warriors returning from the underworld to assist King Waldemar with his latest conflict. We had rehearsed the choral parts for weeks with our choral conductor, but this was our first rehearsal with Ozawa. The score called for the chorus to be seated during the first part of orchestral music. At a certain point in the score, the men's choruses had been instructed to all rise quietly in unison in preparation for our first choral entrance. That is not what Ozawa's orchestra score called for. He was expecting 120 men to jump out of our seats and yell, "Oh-LAAAAAAAH!" at the top of their lungs. When it came time in rehearsal for this event, he gave a huge wind-up like a javelin thrower and threw his arm and baton in the air, and we all rose quietly like a church choir. His knees buckled and he staggered like he had been hit with an anchor punch. He gave us a look as if to say, "WHAT WAS THAT?" The orchestra stopped. When Ozawa regained his composure, he motioned for the choral conductor to approach the podium. They spoke in low tones, so we did not hear what was being said. Ozawa was never one to get upset or speak harshly to anyone, but his body language during this meeting showed this to be the most flustered we ever saw him in years of performances. Rather than trying to fix the entrance then, he decided to resume the rehearsal from the next rehearsal number in the score, allowing us to practice that missed entrance with our choral conductor the next morning. The next morning we practiced enough to get it pretty spectacular for the afternoon rehearsal with Ozawa. In the afternoon rehearsal, he gave us our cue, and we created such a raucous sound that the place shook. The orchestra stopped playing and turned around laughing and gave us a big hand. Ozawa stopped and gave us a big smile of approval. Later that night in the performance, the audience just about jumped out of their seats when we did it.

Ozawa was not one to stand around and chat after rehearsal. An attendant would have his big Mercedes idling at the back gate of Tanglewood. Ozawa would hop in and depart in a cloud of dust and gravel across the huge back parking lot. His time seemed to be carefully scheduled.

Seiji Ozawa was born of Japanese parents in China in 1935. His family returned to Japan after the war, in 1944. Ozawa had studied to be a concert pianist, but that changed when he seriously injured a finger in a rugby game at age 15. This turned out to be a fortuitous event when his teacher took him to a performance of Beethoven's *Fifth Symphony*. From there his intention turned to conducting. By 1960, Ozawa had won a competition in France which resulted in an invitation to study at Tanglewood. From there he was invited to assist Herbert von Karajan at the Berlin Philharmonic, then to assist Leonard Bernstein at the New York Philharmonic. Later, he led the Toronto Symphony from 1965-1969, then the San Francisco Symphony from 1970-1977. His tenure as music director of the Boston Symphony orchestra ran from 1973 – 2002. Then in 2002 he became principal conductor of the Vienna State Opera, a post that he held until 2010. At the same time he had done all this, he had also been a guest conductor for renowned orchestras and opera companies throughout the world. In addition to over 20 international awards, Seiji Ozawa received two Emmys and two Grammys for recordings. He has proven to be one of the world's premier conductors, using his unique talent to enhance the quality of music worldwide.

LUCIANO PAVAROTTI AND MAGDA OLIVERO PERFORM TOGETHER

I N THE 1970'S, PAVAROTTI WAS THE LEADING tenor of the era. I had paid an extravagant amount to get box seats at Symphony Hall once for his recital, because he was my favorite singer. I had listened to recordings of most of the great tenors of the previous decades, and I thought he was the best ever. The beauty and ease of his singing were extraordinary. He was known for his singing, but not for his acting. I read a review once that described Pavarotti as arriving on stage, and after some minimal acknowledgement of the other performers, launching into yet another performance of "The Great Pavarotti."

Magda Olivero, on the other hand, was almost the opposite. She was appreciated for her dramatic singing, but her passionate stage performances were legendary. Reviews typically said that her performances were spellbinding. In 1970, she required police protection after a performance in Turin, Italy, as impassioned fans stormed the stage. The *New York Times* coined the term, "Magda-Maniacs" for her impassioned fans.

Olivero was born in 1910 and started performing in the 1930's. She had one of the longest careers in the history of opera, still performing in the 1990's. For most of her career, she refused to perform outside Europe, so American fans would travel there to see her. In 1975, she relented and traveled to New York for her Metropolitan Opera debut at age 65. Four years later, in 1979, she went on tour with the Met, singing the title role in *Tosca* with Pavarotti. For opera buffs, it was a chance of a lifetime to see and hear these two legends perform together.

The Metropolitan Opera would take several shows on tour each year. Each opera would have a cast, chorus, technical personnel and scenery that would travel for a one-night performance in a major city, then pack up and move to the next city. Right behind that show was another with a different cast and scenery. Thereby, in a specific city, they could show a different opera every night for several nights. As a scene ended, the crew would pack up the scenery into a tractor-trailer truck and the truck would start driving to the next city even before the opera ended. The personnel would take a flight to the next city the following morning.

In the mid-seventies, I was fortunate to have a piano tuning client, Ron, who was the person who hired "Supernumeraries" for the Metropolitan Opera whenever they were on tour in Boston. A "Supernumerary", abbreviated "Super," is the opera term for an "extra." Supernumeraries would be dressed in costume and make-up and would stand around the stage holding spears or looking like hunters, village residents, or whatever characters were needed to set the stage for the opera. They would not sing or speak during the performances. Hiring local people to be Supers allowed the opera company to economize on the cost of touring performances. Over several years, Ron gave me the chance to be in a number of operas.

The Metropolitan Opera management would notify Ron ahead of time as to how many Supers were needed for a particular night, and he would hire his friends at $6 per night. It was so much fun that I would have paid to do it. We arrived at the stage door early, often crossing paths with famous singers. We were put in costume, sent to make-up, and then given about twenty minutes orientation on stage for the location where we would stand and for what actions we should perform. For a person who loves singing, it was an incredible opportunity to be a few feet from major opera stars. Over the years, I heard some of the finest voices in the world, close-up. I was fortunate enough to be invited to take part in the legendary *Tosca* performance of Pavarotti and Olivero.

When the opera personnel oriented us, they would tell us where to stand and what to do, but they did not bother to tell us what the principals would be doing right in front of us. There was a scene early in this performance of *Tosca*, where about twelve of us were standing in line in armor and helmets at the back of the stage on a parapet or castle wall about ten feet above the stage. Each of us held a spear in an upright position next to us. It was a very thin wall, with about six inches of room behind us, and maybe three feet in front of us. We were placed in position before the curtain opened, and our instructions were simply to stand there until the curtain closed for that scene. The curtain opened and as the scene progressed, we were all pretty comfortable and enjoying the view. Then two principals came stomping past us about two inches in front of our noses. They were flinging their arms at each other and having a loud disagreement. The castle wall started swaying forward and backward and seemed destined for collapse. Our knees were buckling as we swayed forward and back, trying to stay on top of the wall. My mind flashed to the fact that this scenery folded up easily for transport. I stole a quick look at the guy next to me and saw him glancing over his shoulder at the stage floor behind us about ten feet down. It looked like he was trying to decide whether to jump, or to just wait it out and fall with the rest of us. It seems funny now, as I recall it, but we were terrified at the time. Somehow, the parapet gradually stopped swaying, and we regained our composure.

In the course of this performance with Pavarotti and Olivero, I was required to prepare for several scenes in different costumes, so unfortunately I was not able to experience the dramatic effect of Olivero's performance. I think I would have needed to be in the audience for the whole performance to have gotten the full effect.

I did get to see one important scene, however. The score calls for Tosca to leap to her death off the parapet at the back of the stage when she discovers the death of her lover. She would land on some soft cushion out of the view of the audience, but it still would be a risky move. There was some speculation among the Supers as to whether Olivero would really do it at age 69. As a result, there was a small gathering of Supers back stage to see the end of the opera, and sure enough, true to her legend for drama, she jumped.

My main priority for the evening had been to hear

Pavarotti, and I was not disappointed. I had performed around many of the top voices of the day, and I could usually hear at least some strain in every other singer's voice. I did not perceive that at all with Pavarotti, though. I knew he was extremely well-versed in technique and that he was very much consciously controlling his breath and voice, but it appeared to be completely effortless. It seemed as though he just stood there and opened his mouth, and a voice came straight down from heaven. There was no strain perceivable in the sound of his voice. I had never heard anything like it, and I never have since. It was a deeply-moving experience of a resounding depth and beauty in music that one rarely hears, and it's one that I'll never forget.

Singing in the Mahler *Second Symphony* at Carnegie Hall

T HE MAHLER SOCIETY OF NEW YORK IS AN organization dedicated to promoting and performing the works of Gustav Mahler, an often-overlooked composer. Mahler was a Late Romantic composer who bridged the period from the 19th century to the modern era. He was a full-time orchestra and opera conductor, and a part-time composer. Throughout his entire career, he faced criticism from a hostile anti-semitic press, even as early as the 1890's. Later, in the Nazi era, his music was banned from German-held regions, and it was not widely played for two decades after the Second World War. In 1976 a small group of New Yorkers founded The Mahler Society of New York to restore his work to the public awareness. Similar organizations have sprung up around the world, and Mahler's work is again being performed regularly.

In 1980, the Mahler Society of New York contracted

with the Boston Philharmonic and the Chorus Pro Musica of Boston to present Mahler's *Second Symphony* at Carnegie Hall in New York. At the time, I was a member of the Chorus Pro Musica, and I was familiar with the Boston Philharmonic, since the chorus often hired the orchestra for large performances.

There were several things that made the Boston Philharmonic Orchestra especially interesting. They were an amateur group, conducted by Ben Zander, of New England Conservatory. Zander had been a protege of Benjamin Britten, and had won numerous awards prior to arriving in Boston. It was widely believed that he could conduct a major orchestra if he wished, but he chose to teach and conduct amateurs, because he found it to be more satisfying and rewarding. I understood his motivation. These spirited amateurs brought life to their music by playing at the limit of their capability much of the time. This made for some lively and exciting performances.

Most of the orchestra members were students from New England Conservatory and Boston Conservatory, but some were older amateur musicians. Their commitment and enthusiasm can be illustrated by a story Zander related to us. He told of an elderly second violinist who called Zander on the phone one winter afternoon. The violinist was very upset that he would be missing that evening's rehearsal because of his wife's illness. He hadn't missed a rehearsal in eighteen years. It turned out there was a blizzard that night and the rehearsal was cancelled, so he didn't miss after all.

Word had it that the middle-aged tympanist, Earl, was a former professional who had been fired from other orchestras, because he was so difficult to manage. He would have outbursts in the middle of rehearsals, arguing with Zander openly. Zander was able to handle him so that the orchestra could use his immense talent. Not many conductors would have bothered, but boy, did it pay off. Earl was absolutely brilliant as a musician and perfect for the *Mahler Second*, since it requires a flamboyant and flawless tympanist for many featured parts. The intensity of his playing strengthened the whole performance. You could close your eyes and imagine a muppet banging on the tympani with all his might, perfectly in time, driving the music forward.

We were in the the midst of rehearsing when it became obvious that the soprano soloist needed to be replaced. She was somewhat well-known, but so far past her prime that she could not sing the music adequately. Two weeks before the performance Zander auditioned women from the chorus for the part. One young woman was chosen and she sang like an angel.

Another important point about the *Mahler Second* is that it is not a symphony to be played by amateurs. The complexity, difficulty, and passion of the music virtually requires professionals. It calls for an enormous orchestra with a huge percussion section, a chorus, and four vocal soloists. It would be a major undertaking for the conductor, Ben Zander, to hold together all the different parts of this performance. It was fascinating to watch how many things he had to manage at once.

At the dress rehearsal, I remember sitting on stage waiting for a choral section, as the contralto sang her solo. Her singing was so beautiful that it brought tears to my eyes. I don't recall that ever happening to me at a rehearsal. At any rate, I looked to my left, and the guy next to me had tears in his eyes, too. It made me wonder, so I glanced to my right and saw the same thing happening with the guy next to me. Sometimes magic just happens unpredictably.

I had invited my mother to the performance, and she jumped at the chance. Back in the 1930's, my mother's New York voice teacher had once rented the small upstairs recital hall at Carnegie for the recital of her students, and my mother was proud to have sung there as a young woman. It would be a big deal for her to see me sing in the large hall, even if it were just as part of a chorus. She took the train from Delaware for the concert and brought along her older sister, my Aunt Clara, who was visiting from Seattle.

When the chorus took the stage for the dress rehearsal, I saw Mom and Aunt Clara sitting half-way back in the empty hall. They had taken the train, then the subway across town, and had somehow slipped in at the stage door. After rehearsal, I had a small window of time and I met up with both of them. We walked in Central Park and stopped to sit on a bench together and talk, just the three of us. Aunt Clara was the definition of an iconoclast. She always had a fresh way of looking at things that was not usually the approved point of view. In the 1930's she drove a red roadster with a rumble seat. She was a school librarian, and did not marry until she was in her fifties. She always counseled me to try new things, saying that that would keep me young. I had a lot of affection for her, and I always found her fun to be around. She did not have any children of her own, so she was always looking out for all her nieces and nephews, of which there were fifteen. Mom and I did not get to see her very often, since she lived across the continent, so we all had a great time visiting. While we were sitting on that bench in Central Park, Aunt Clara stopped a passer-by and had him take our picture with her camera.

At the performance that evening, Ben Zander was in complete command. The music was beautiful and exciting, but the thing I remember most was how amazed I was that he had no trouble managing all the disparate parts of the performance so that a beautiful musical experience resulted. The New York Mahler Society members were very pleased.

Seventeen years later, Mom showed me the picture of her, Aunt Clara, and me sitting on a bench in Central Park. The picture had arrived as part of Aunt Clara's belongings, after she passed away. Mom couldn't remember where it was taken, so I reminded her about that afternoon near Carnegie Hall that was so special to the three of us.

Steinway, Steinert, Hume, and *Hamlet*

WHEN I WAS IN MY 30'S, I WAS LIVING IN Lexington, Massachusetts, northwest of Boston. A friend of mine, Carol, who was a choreographer, invited me to audition to be a dancer in a community theater production of *My Fair Lady*. Previously, I had danced in a production of hers as a last minute fill-in. I had been tuning the piano for the opening of that previous show, and Carol wasn't happy with one of the dance numbers. She had choreographed a scene with a line of eight women tap dancers dressed in black tails, black leotards, fishnet stockings, and top hats. For appearances, she decided she wanted one male dancer in the middle of the line of dancers. We were talking and she asked me if I could tap. I never had, but I was a musician and a soccer player, so I had the strength and the ability. Also, I owned a black tuxedo, which was crucial. She taught me the routine, then had me wear soft shoes in case I made a mistake. I danced well enough to fake it, because everyone in the audience was looking at all those women's legs anyway. The dance scene in that previous show was successful enough that Carol remembered me the following year when she needed a dancer for *My Fair Lady*.

For *My Fair Lady*, I would be auditioning to be in the broom dance scene. I walked into the audition and Carol introduced me to the director. He immediately said, "Oh! You look just like Freddy, and we don't have a Freddy. Can you sing?" Freddy is the character who sings the song, "On the Street Where You Live." I sang the song for them and I was no longer a dancer; I was cast as a principal character. You couldn't ask for a better role in a show. I had a great song to perform, my costumes were attractive, I got to speak in an aristocratic accent, and I didn't have to memorize a lot of speaking lines. On top of all that, the cast was filled with lovely single women.

There was one young woman in particular that I got along with well. She had just graduated from an elite women's college in western New England and she had moved back in with her parents while she was in transition between school and finding a job.

We always had a great time together, and eventually our friendship developed into a relationship. Her name was Currier, after one of the founders of Currier and Ives. She and her twin sister had been adopted as infants, and her adoptive parents were very proud of their New England heritage. As a result, family activities were always done in a proper traditional New England manner.

For example, I was invited to join the family on their boat on the Charles River to watch the Fourth of July fireworks at the Hatch Shell in Boston when the Boston Pops played. On the boat, we were served salmon and fresh peas, which they explained, was the traditional New England Fourth of July dinner.

Another time, I was visiting Currier at her home one evening, and mention was made of the Steinway piano in an adjoining room. The mother asked if I would like to see it. You'll probably enjoy the story more if I give you a little more background information about pianos before I proceed with the story.

When I worked at the Steinway franchise early in my career, the son of the owner told me the following story about piano making at the turn of the 20th century: The name of the Steinway franchise in Boston was *Steinert's,* a name similar to *Steinway,* but only by coincidence. The families were not related. Steinert's had wanted to make their own piano in the early 20th century, but Steinway objected to the similarity of the names, claiming infringement on their trademark. They threatened to withdraw the Steinway franchise unless Steinert's gave their piano a different name. Steinert's acquiesced to their demands and named the piano after their plant manager, Mr. Hume.

Hume pianos were made from 1903 to 1916 and marketed all over New England. Even in small towns that did not have a piano store, Steinert's would send a boxcar full of pianos. A salesman was left with the boxcar on a siding. He would sell the pianos right out of the boxcar, without need of a storefront. That's how popular pianos were at that time. There was no radio yet, so pianos were the principal form of entertainment in American homes. Thousands of children were required to learn to play the piano, in order to entertain their family and guests. Manufacturers couldn't make pianos fast enough to keep up with the demand. The Hume piano company, however, was not as profitable as Steinert's had expected. After thirteen years of producing pianos and not making much profit, Steinert's decided to look at the account books a little more closely.

It turned out that the Hume Piano Company had manufactured a lot more pianos than were reported as being sold on the books. Another way of saying it is that Mr. Hume was "cooking the books." He was selling pianos on the side and keeping the proceeds himself. It was probably very easy to have the bank drafts made out to Hume and to just deposit them into his personal account. Steinert's never prosecuted him, but he was fired with malice. After this, of course, the brand name of the piano needed to be changed. After discussions, Steinway relented on their objections to the Steinert name, and the Steinert piano was born. It was produced from 1916 until the depression, in 1930, when most piano makers went under. People who owned a Steinert piano often thought that they owned a Steinway product, similar to Lexus owners having a car made by Toyota. The Steinert piano was a very close copy of a Steinway, but they were independent companies.

One question, though, was what to do with all those Hume pianos out in the world. The Steinert family was so angry at being defrauded by Mr. Hume that for decades they bought used Hume pianos whenever they came on the market. They brought them into the shop, changed the name, and then resold them as Steinert pianos. They changed the name by replacing the Hume decal on the key cover with a Steinert decal, but there was a problem with the Hume name cast into the iron plate that runs the length of each piano. You could not replace a plate without rebuilding the whole piano, so they just ground the Hume name off the cast iron plate and repainted it to look as if there had never been a brand name there.

By the time I met Currier, I had seen all three possibilities. I had tuned Hume pianos that still had their original name, I had tuned Hume pianos whose names had been changed to Steinert, and I had tuned genuine Steinert pianos that were made after 1916 with the name "Steinert" cast into the plates.

Now, resuming my story back at Currier's house, I approached what her parents thought was a Steinway piano and I found a *Steinert* decal on the key cover. I lifted the lid and stared at a blank spot on the plate where a brand name should have been cast. Not only did they not have a Steinway, they didn't even have a Steinert. They had a Hume. To me, that was exciting and interesting. I thought it would be great to own a piano with such a colorful history. I failed to look at it from the parents' point of view, however, so stupid me, I told them. The parents were not amused. For them, their piano had been a status item that they had exhibited to numerous friends, and no amount of interesting history could make up for the loss of status and the potential embarrassment.

This new information about their piano put a strain on my relationship with the parents, and it was not long until my relationship with Currier ended. It had been a pleasant relationship, though, and I have sweet memories of fun days at the beach, of being in *My Fair Lady* together, and of watching the fireworks on the Charles River on the Fourth of July.

The events surrounding the Hume piano gave me a greater appreciation for my favorite passage in *Hamlet*: When Laertes is leaving for France, his father, Polonius, gives him advice in one of the best-known speeches in English literature, which includes this guidance,

"Give every man thine ear, but few thy voice."

Because of the consequences with Currier's family when I didn't follow that advice, I learned to be more careful in expressing my opinion about my clients' pianos, and that has saved me many times in the decades that have followed.

AMAHL AND THE NIGHT VISITORS

DURING THE COMMUNITY THEATER PRO-duction of *My Fair Lady*, I developed a friendship with Roger, the gentleman who played Alfie Doolittle, the father of Eliza Doolittle. Alfie is the character in *My Fair Lady* who sings the song, "Get me to the Church on Time."

Roger was a voice teacher who also directed the church choir at a small historic church in the affluent suburbs west of Boston. His wife Evelyn taught piano, and she was an extraordinary pianist. She also played the organ at the church where Roger directed. They had an eleven-year-old son, Phillip, who played violin, and he was also a tremendous talent as a boy soprano.

A few weeks after the conclusion of the production of *My Fair Lady*, Roger and Evelyn hired me to tune their two home pianos. As a result of spending time in their home, I was able to get to know them a little better. Evelyn told me that Phillip was not her first child. She also had two boys with her first husband, but that marriage ended in a divorce. Sadly, after the divorce Evelyn's first husband kidnapped the children and they disappeared for ten years. She spent a good deal of time and money searching for them, and eventually the authorities found them living in rural Maine. Having been kept in captivity by their father, the boys had never been to school, so they could barely read or write, and they had no experience of the outside world.

As a result of what had happened to Evelyn's first two boys, Roger and Evelyn treasured their son, Phillip. They gave him the best education and every opportunity they could provide. The high vocal range of a boy soprano's voice lasts only until puberty, so Roger and Evelyn decided to give Phillip an opportunity to display his talent before his voice changed. They gathered their resources together and mounted a small production of *Amahl and the Night Visitors* in the function room of their church. The show would feature Phillip as the boy-soprano lead, playing the role of Amahl.

Amahl and the Night Visitors was a highly acclaimed short opera by Menotti that was written specifically for production on television. From 1951 to 1966, a live performance of it was televised each year at Christmas time. The original performance, on Christmas eve, 1951, had a television audience of nearly 5 million. The annual television performances were widely watched by American families for 15 years. Although the opera is not very well known these days, it is a very interesting and beautiful piece of music and drama.

In the story, the main character, Amahl, is a twelve-year-old crippled shepherd boy, known for his tall tales, who lives in a hut with his widowed mother. Because of Amahl's progressing disability, he has become unable to herd their sheep and the mother has recently been forced to sell them. As a result, Amahl and his mother are presently out of resources and are left only to beg for food. Three wise men, who are traveling on a journey to bring valuable gifts to a newborn king, stop at their home and ask for shelter for the night. The mother graciously offers them a bed of straw.

While visiting with them, the kings sing a trio describing all the wonderful traits of the child they are seeking. The mother sings an answer, as if to herself, that she knows such a child with all those wonderful traits, and it is her son, Amahl.

However, the kings do not acknowledge what she sings, and they continue to carry on about all the wonderful characteristics of this child they are looking for. The mother answers every verse, singing that her son has all those qualities, and that although he is poor and hungry, no one is bringing him valuable gifts.

Later on in the middle of the night, the mother is tempted to try to steal some of their gold, but she is caught. The kings confer, and they decide to let her keep a small amount of the gold. They continue to persevere in singing about the importance of this child they seek, and Amahl is inspired to offer the newborn child his only possession, his crutch. When he does that, a miracle occurs, and he can walk again. Great joy and dancing ensues for the finale, and the opera concludes with Amahl deciding to accompany the kings to worship the newborn child.

The show requires only a small cast, but the music is very demanding. Roger and Evelyn joined together with some of their musician friends and they rehearsed the show for a few weeks, in preparation for a December performance on a small stage in the function room at their church. Evelyn played the entire score on the piano, which was not an easy feat, and Roger played one of the wise men. I was invited to sing in the chorus.

It was a small production with less than a hundred people in the audience, but it was pure enchantment. You can never predict when a performance will somehow transform into something very special, but this was one of those times. Phillip sang like an angel, and the woman playing his mother was remarkable. The wise men carried off their trio beautifully, and Evelyn played the very difficult score flawlessly. The end result was a truly dramatic effect that was far more than the sum of the parts. The experience was very moving, emotionally, for everyone who was involved.

For being such a small production, the show required a significant amount of work to prepare and to produce. There is something very gratifying about expending extraordinary effort simply to produce something beautiful. We all knew Phillip's voice would change sometime soon, so we knew we only had one chance. Without having an extraordinary talent to play Amahl, we could never do such a performance again. And we were all very thankful we had taken the opportunity.

An Evening
with the San
Jose Symphony

IN 1987, I PULLED UP STAKES IN BOSTON AND moved to San Jose, California. I had originally moved to Boston because I loved snow, but after 14 years of cold and wet, I was ready for a change. Additionally, as a teenager, I had read skateboard and surfing magazines and dreamed of living in sunny California, so I thought I'd give it a try.

I rented a house in Cupertino, a suburb of San Jose, where Apple Computer was based, and I started a piano tuning business by tuning for a piano dealership located there. I had an agreement with the owner of the piano store that whenever I was sent out to tune a customer's newly purchased piano, I could leave my business card with the client in hopes that they would hire me directly for subsequent tunings. In this manner, I gradually built up my piano tuning business.

I wanted to continue with my choral singing, so in the fall of 1996 I joined the San Jose Symphony chorus. The

San Jose Symphony was the oldest continuously operated symphony orchestra in California. At that time, it was not the quality of the San Francisco Symphony, but it was very good. The conductor was a respected Russian-born and trained musician. One reason I joined the chorus that year was because of the repertoire they were performing. In the fall we sang the Mahler *Second Symphony*, which is one of my favorites, and in the spring we sang the Brahms *German Requiem*, which is a wonderful piece that I somehow had never sung before, except at an informal summer sing with the Chorus Pro Musica in Boston.

The choral director of the San Jose Symphony Chorus was relatively young and inexperienced, so she had a tendency to over-rehearse right before the concerts, leaving us quite exhausted. The week that we rehearsed and performed the Brahms *Requiem* was particularly grueling. Starting Tuesday night, we sang two to three hours per night at rehearsals. After a long dress rehearsal on Thursday night, the chorus manager discovered that she had not arranged the seating of the chorus properly. As a result, the chorus had to stay an additional hour longer on a week night, after working all day and singing all evening.

The next night, Friday, was our opening night. Instead of simply warming up, we rehearsed for an hour before the curtains opened, so we were already tired by the start of the concert. The performance went well for the first hour or so, but then things began to unravel.

About a minute before a major full-voice entrance of the chorus, the well-known baritone was finishing a solo singing the words in German, "The last trumpet shall sound!" At that very instant, a soprano, who was standing in the front row center of the chorus, fainted. She did not crumple quietly to the riser. She basically took a swan-dive forward off the four-foot-high riser and took out the third trumpet player and his music stand, with an enormous crash. The orchestra conductor must have been looking in another direction at the time, because he did not see this happen. He likely assumed that some equipment had fallen, so he simply continued to beat time. He leaned to each side, trying to see what the problem was, but the two people were on the floor at the back of the orchestra, hidden from his view.

The chorus, meanwhile got distracted watching the people on the floor, and we lost track of where we were in the music. Soon it came time for the huge entrance of 120 voices at full volume. The conductor wound up and gave a big cue for this mighty entrance, and all of us looked up startled and disoriented as to where we were in the music. No sound came from the chorus.

I've never seen a conductor's face turn that pale that fast. It didn't seem real. I thought he would stop, so the woman could be cared for, and then we would restart. He still didn't know what had happened, though, so somehow he continued to beat time, the orchestra continued to play, and members of the chorus gradually found their places and started singing. A couple of stage hands picked up the unconscious woman and carried her off the stage as we all sang in German, "The dead shall be resurrected. Death where is thy sting? Hell, where is thy fury?" I know it sounds like I made this up. This was one of those times in life when things happen that if you made it up, no one would believe it.

Eventually things came back together and the concert proceeded. Soon it was time for the next entrance of the baritone soloist. He had been up at the front of the stage singing when that unnerving crash took place, but he was unable to turn around to see what had happened. He was so distracted by it that he had gone back to his seat on the stage and closed his music, completely forgetting that he still had more to sing. When it came time for his entrance, the conductor turned and gave him a big cue for his entrance, but he wasn't even standing there. Instead, he was across the stage sitting down, relaxing.

This time we got a profile view of the conductor's face as it turned ashen. Twice within five minutes he had given big cues for entrances, and nobody was home. It was starting to feel like a Bugs Bunny cartoon, when they would make fun of opera scenes. I could see Bugs up on the podium having all the color drain out of his face as things fell apart. To get the baritone's attention, the conductor turned toward him and started singing his part. The baritone jumped out of his seat, started thumbing through his music, and began making up stuff in German-sounding syllables until he found his place.

That was how the loud crashing sixth movement of the piece went. It was followed by the quiet, beautiful last movement of the *Requiem*. The chorus was largely able to regroup for this movement. We were distracted enough that there were a few bad entrances, but nothing dramatic.

At the end, I thought we would have to duck and cover to get out of there alive. An Italian audience would have turned us into tomato sauce. The kind people of San Jose, however, rewarded our perseverance by giving us a standing ovation and curtain calls. By the second curtain call, even the conductor was able to manage a slight smile.

Tuning for *The Mentalist* TV Program

IN 2004, I MOVED FROM NORTHERN California to Los Angeles to start a new life with my fiancée, and it was one of the best things I have ever done. Our relationship has been wonderful, and I found that there is a huge demand for piano tuning in Los Angeles. I think the shortage of piano tuners in the area is the result of LA having such an overwhelming reputation for cinema. Piano tuners in other parts of the country don't realize there is a lot of focus on music in LA, so they don't think of moving to the area. In fact, Los Angeles, is a musical epicenter. Besides the many recording studios, musical theaters, performing arts centers, voice and piano teachers, there are also several universities in the area with extraordinary music departments.

Also, internet advertising made starting a piano tuning business much easier for me than it had ever been before. I soon had a website, and my fiancée knew everything about how to advertise on the Internet, so I had plenty of tuning work immediately. Gone were the days of working at a piano dealer for years in order to build a tuning business.

One morning a fellow from Warner Brothers saw my website ad online, and he called me in a panic, saying that he needed a piano tuned immediately for filming. I hadn't been to Warner Brothers before, so I thought it would be a fun experience. I rearranged my work schedule, and I drove right over. Two of their employees greeted me at the gate, and invited me to join them in their golf cart. They drove me over to the set location for the filming of a TV program called *The Mentalist*. They introduced me to the director as a rehearsal of a scene was going on. The area was not like a stage set. Instead, it was an entire house with a very old grand piano in the living room.

I was told that the piano had been rented and delivered just for that day's filming. When they rented it, they must have specified that the piano should look old, but evidently they failed to specify that it should function as a working piano. As a result, the piano company had sent over a stage prop that hadn't worked in decades. The script called for an actress to play the piano in one scene, and they had planned to start filming that scene in three hours. I tried to play the piano and it was a complete wreck. Numerous keys stuck down when they were played, and individual notes were wildly out of tune. When individual notes are way out of tune, it usually means that the tuning pins are loose. Tightening or replacing tuning pins, however, would take longer than the time I had available before the filming.

I told the director that I needed to take a few minutes to assess the condition of the piano to see if it could be made playable within the necessary time frame, or whether they might need to rent another piano quickly. The whole time I was tearing this piano apart, there was a rehearsal going on around me, with actors emoting and camera crews following the action around the rooms and up and down stairways. It was a significantly different experience than my usual home tunings.

I checked the tuning pins, and they were tight enough to hold the string tension for the minimal playing that was planned. The bigger problem was that the key leads had come loose and had walked their way out of the sides of the keys. The leads of numerous keys were hitting the leads of their neighboring keys, so that their movement was restricted.

To explain more about this, small cylinders of lead are put in piano keys as one of the last steps in the manufacture of a piano action. The process is called "weighing off the action." The purpose is to have each of the keys require the same specific amount of force to be played so that the performer has the best control of the volume when they are playing. That process gives the performer the opportunity to play expressively. If the touch of a piano were to vary from note to note, then certain notes would be louder or softer than others and the performer could not know what to expect. Occasionally, these leads come loose, but usually they just rattle a little when they do. It is extremely rare for so many leads to work their way out to the point of disrupting the functioning of the keys.

Fortunately, the actress who was going to play the piano arrived early, and she showed me the piece she was going to play. I believe it was a minuet from the *Notebook for Anna Magdalena Bach*. I noted the exact range of the piece so that I could tune and fix only the notes she was going to play. This way I wouldn't waste time tuning and repairing notes above and below the range that would be used. I reported to the director that I could not get the piano concert-ready, but that I could get it to function minimally so it would sound like a poorly maintained home piano. He said that was good enough, but he needed to immediately film a scene in the room where the piano was located.

I was told to take a break for an hour and to come back at noon while the cast and crew would be taking their lunch break. During that time, I would have an hour to tune and repair the piano. I had been hoping to have at least two hours for the work. To do it all in one hour was going to be a challenge. Normally it takes almost an hour just to tune a piano when it is only slightly out of tune, and this piano was significantly out of tune. I had figured that the repairs I needed to do would take about an hour, as well. The good thing was that I needed to tune and repair only about half the piano, the middle section, for the specific piece that would be played. I told the director I'd give it a try. While they filmed, I went off to the commissary for my break. I needed to eat immediately, because it might be a while before I would get another chance.

My lunch at the commissary reminded me of the end of *Blazing Saddles*, the Mel Brooks movie, when all the outlandishly costumed actors from different movies are having lunch together at the Warner Brothers commissary and an enormous food fight erupts. There weren't that many unusual costumes when I was there, because the type of films made these days use mostly modern dress. There was no food fight that day, either, but it was still fun to imagine what happened in that movie as I had lunch with all the "Industry" personnel. In Los Angeles, one speaks of the entertainment industry simply as "The Industry," as if there were no other industries in Los Angeles.

By 11:55 a.m. I was standing outside the door of *The Mentalist* house with two of my tools cases, ready to go. Thank goodness I knew the range of the piece that would be played. I began by tuning those notes and a few extra above and below the range of the piece as fast as I could move my tuning hammer. Next, I pulled the keyboard and action out and put it up on top of the piano. After that, I removed the top part of the action, called the "stack," so that I could access the individual keys. I removed each malfunctioning key and pounded the leads back into place and tightened them so that they wouldn't come out again. I replaced the stack and then I fixed a few other malfunctioning action parts.

I had placed my watch on the piano in front of me so that I could monitor the time. I learned years ago that human intention is very powerful when it comes to managing time. I can intend for something to occur in a specified amount of time and often it miraculously does. Still, I was working as fast as I could. When all the malfunctioning parts had been repaired, I slid the keyboard and action back into place. Then I secured the key blocks, the key slip, and the key cover. I put the music desk in place, and I tested the piano. It played adequately in the range that was needed. I suddenly wished I had memorized the piano part to *There's No Business Like Show Business*, so I could have played it at that moment. Subsequently I did memorize it, and it has been a lot of fun to play it when I have prepared a piano for a stage or film performance and there are a lot of performers standing around.

It was 12:57 pm and I was scheduled to finish at 1:00 pm. At that moment, I was startled by a voice from behind me asking me if I was finished. I didn't realize that the stage crew had been standing there, ready to move the piano into place for the scene. They had come back from lunch earlier than the performers, so that they could put everything in the proper places for filming. I had time to visit with them a little as they worked, and they were delightful people. They were much more upbeat than the performers who had been waiting around the periphery of the set all morning waiting for their cues. I had often imagined that it was a romantic life being an actor, but most of the performers that I saw that day looked pretty unhappy, as they stood around waiting for their cues. It was all the surrounding crews that seemed to be enjoying themselves.

I have often wished that I had stayed to watch the filming, but I had other piano tuning appointments scheduled that day. I don't know if anyone in the production appreciated what a miracle it was to get that piano working again that fast, but it was quite satisfying for me to accomplish such a demanding undertaking. I would say it was a little like running the 100-yard dash while saving a sinking ship. On the other hand, at Warner Brothers and other Hollywood studios, too, I'm sure they deal with situations like this one every day, where people are somehow making things work just in the nick of time for filming. It's probably a common occurrence in "The Industry."

WALT DISNEY'S PIANO

IN JULY OF 2011, I RECEIVED A CALL FROM
the director of the Walt Disney Archives in Burbank.
Walt Disney's personal office piano had arrived from
Anaheim, and it was scheduled to be played within a few
days. The piano needed to be tuned and serviced right away.

Walt Disney Studios produces many of their movies
at a large facility in Burbank at the corner of Buena Vista
and Alameda. Most people in the area have noticed the
brightly colored, vertically-striped building bearing the
word, "Animation," as they drive along the 134 freeway
in Burbank. The compound contains numerous buildings, including one with giant statues of the Seven Dwarfs
seemingly holding up the roof of the two-story structure.

I had previously tuned two other pianos at Disney Studios, but I had never seen Disney's personal piano, which
had been in his office. On the day I was scheduled to
tune it, I drove along the freeway wondering what brand
of piano Disney would have owned. Maybe a Mason &
Hamlin, or perhaps a Steinway. I knew, though, that it
might be anything. I had previously tuned what was pur-
ported to be Charlie Chaplin's piano, and it was a good
brand, but not the best known. It was custom made by a

The Seven Dwarfs holding up a roof at Disney Studios

small family-owned company that had the flexibility to make special-order pianos for celebrities.

I had been instructed to go to the Disney Archives Department in the Frank G. Wells Building, across the plaza from the building with the enormous statues of the Seven Dwarfs holding up the roof. The Disney Archives is a large department. A staff person escorted me to the room where Disney's piano was stored. As we walked through rooms of memorabilia, I saw cases holding Academy Awards, Emmys, and People's Choice award statuettes. There were also rows of costumes and shelves holding props from movies and TV programs. Davy Crocket's coonskin cap was there, for example. I had one just like it in the 1950's. You might think only of animation with Disney, but they made quite a few movies using people, such as *Mary Poppins*. There was a huge room of files that looked like the Library of Congress, where you could turn a wheel, and the entire aisle of files would slowly move to one side to make room to walk down along the side of the structure to access a file. I was reminded of the priceless nature of all this memorabilia when I was told that I would be accompanied at all times while I was in the archives.

When I first saw Walt Disney's piano, I was a little disappointed. It wasn't until I looked at it more carefully that I found it interesting. It was a 1914 Knabe grand piano with a mahogany case and unusual legs and lyre. The lyre is the wooden structure under the piano that houses the pedals. Knabe pianos are not among the best-known brands today, but they were highly regarded in that era. They were the official piano of the Metropolitan Opera Company, for example. When this piano was made in 1914, their factory was in Baltimore. They are considered to be one of the top four American piano builders of that era. The other three were Steinway, Mason and Hamlin, and Baldwin. Knabe built solid pianos that held a tuning very well.

I was told that this piano had recently been moved to the archives from storage in Anaheim, and that nothing was known about it. I was asked to report on the condition and on anything else I could discern about the instrument.

I started my examination by lifting the lid. I could see that the stringing was original and was rusted. The bass strings sounded "tubby," which is common with bass strings of that age. The treble bridge had numerous hair-line cracks, and the soundboard had a hair-line crack. The pin block was in good shape, though, so all the tuning pins were tight enough to hold a tuning. The tone was very uneven, with some notes jumping out at you, louder than their surrounding notes. The action was quite worn, but the hammers had enough felt on them that they

The author with Walt Disney's piano in Disney's newly restored office

could be filed, which would help improve the beauty and evenness of the tone. The keyboard, on the other hand was almost flawless. There was only one ivory key cover with a hair-line crack. Otherwise, it was a perfect ivory keyboard, which is rare. The veneer on the top of the piano was significantly damaged, though. It looked like someone had left a potted plant on it for years without noticing that the moisture was ruining the veneer.

It was the piano case which I found most interesting. It took me quite a while to figure out whether the piano was original, or whether it had been modified. The piano had a mahogany case with matching art deco mahogany legs that were 21" wide and 4" thick, with rounded ends, so they would have looked elliptical if seen in cross-section. There was a black trim detail across the front of the piano, just below the keys. The black trim went around the sides of the piano and down the rear edge of the front legs, linking the whole design together so that it looked like the legs were original. The problem was that the art deco style of the legs was 1920's-1930's, yet the piano serial number dated the original manufacture of the piano as 1914. I could not imagine anyone going to all that trouble to modify a piano to get that appearance, and I had never seen a modification that was done that well. Typically, celebrities would special order a case from the manufacturer, so that the piano would be made to their specifications from the start. The legs on Disney's piano matched the color of the veneer of the piano perfectly, as if they were original, but their style was too modern. I was stumped at first.

One clue was that the lyre was definitely not original. It was sharply rectangular and was painted salmon on some of its surfaces. The same salmon color was painted on the underside of the lid. It was obvious that at least some of the piano had been modified, but the legs matched so well that it was hard to believe they were not original.

I took out my high-intensity light to look at the legs more carefully. The tail leg had mahogany veneer whose grain matched the grain on the body of the piano. The treble and bass legs, however, even though they matched the color perfectly, had a different grain with more swirls suggestive of a walnut veneer. It was starting to look like the legs were a later modification. As I thought about it, the original finish on a 1914 piano would have been varnish. This finish was lacquer, so the whole piano had definitely been stripped and refinished. At the time of refinishing, it would have been easy to use the same stain on the modified legs, so that they matched the color of the body of the piano.

Close-up of the black trim on Walt Disney's piano

The one thing I still could not explain was the black trim that ran across the front of the piano and down the legs. It was installed so perfectly that it looked original. Yet, it could not have been original with different shaped legs, as it was an integral part of both the piano legs and the case.

The question was answered when I started to slide out the action of the piano. The black trim was flush with the *bottom* of the keybed, so that it looked perfect when the piano was assembled; however, once the keyslip (the thin piece of wood in front of the keys) was removed, I could see that the top of the trim was slightly above the level of the *top* of the keybed. That is significant, because it created a lip at the front edge of the keybed, so that the action could not be easily removed. No piano maker would make that mistake. Only a cabinet maker who did not thoroughly know pianos would have done that. It was proof that the trim and the legs were a modification. Apparently the piano's appearance was modified by a very skilled cabinet maker, so that the piano coordinated with the art deco style of the rest of Walt Disney's office decor. I later wrote up my findings, and submitted them to the archives department for their records.

Placed in the controlled temperature and humidity of the archives, the piano will probably last another 60-100 years. I was able to tune it, partially regulate the action, and voice it (to even out the tone) in time for its intended use that week by Richard Sherman. The archives director informed me that Richard Sherman and his brother Robert wrote the music for many Disney classics, including *Mary Poppins*, and "It's a Small World" at Disneyland. When Disney was alive, Richard Sherman would visit him every Friday afternoon and play songs for him on the piano. Usually Disney would ask for his favorite song, "Feed the Birds" from *Mary Poppins*. Disney did not play piano himself, but since 1939 every song for every production was auditioned on this piano so that Disney could make the final choices of which songs would be included.

Russell Schroeder, author of *Disney's Lost Chords*, pointed out that music was an essential part of Disney films, and was taken very seriously. Disney hired award-winning song writers for his films. For example, imagine *Pinocchio* without "When you Wish upon a Star,'" or *Snow White* without "Someday my Prince will Come" and "Whistle While You Work."

Disney's Lost Chords are two large coffee table style limited edition volumes containing songs and animation that had been cut from Disney movies. When Disney movies were being prepared, there were always more songs commissioned than were finally needed. There are hundreds of songs in the Disney archives. The songs and their accompanying animation usually had been cut at the last minute if they were not essential for the story line. For example, in *Snow White and the Seven Dwarfs*, the movie was too long and was over budget by a factor of three. As a result, a song called "You're Never Too Old to be Young," was cut. It was published for the first time in *Disney's Lost Chords*, with accompanying illustrations and explanation. The author of the book, Russell Schroeder, explained that of the hundreds of songs in the archives, only a few dozen could be chosen for his books.

I had previously been given the two-volume set in appreciation for my tuning at another Disney animation facility in Glendale, the next town over from Burbank. For two years in a row, they had forgotten to schedule a tuning before their Christmas party, so they appreciated that I tuned for them on short notice.

Looking through Schroeder's books, I found a picture of Walt Disney standing in front of the Knabe piano, with a quotation saying that for him, the music was an integral part of every story.

A few weeks after I tuned Disney's piano, I received an email from the director of the archives. They had found a write-up about the piano from a 1941 magazine called *California Arts and Architecture*.

The article reported that Disney wanted a piano that would fit into the decor of his new office. Rather than purchase a specially made piano, the studio purchased a used piano from a mover's warehouse. They then had

Kem Weber, a supervising designer, modify and refinish the piano case to suit the office design.

After reading this, I looked up Kem Weber on the internet, and found out that he was best known for being the chief architect for the Disney Studios. His earliest training, however, was in Germany as a cabinet maker, rather than as an architect. It makes perfect sense, then, that he could perform such flawless work on the case of Walt Disney's piano.

One year later, in June of 2012, the piano was moved out to the Reagan Library in Simi Valley, California for a temporary exhibit of Disney memorabilia. Disney personnel recreated Disney's original office complete with an image of the view that would have been seen from his Burbank office window. I was hired to tune the piano after it was moved to the library, so that it would be ready for Richard Sherman to play it. After the 6-month exhibit, the piano was moved back to the archives in Burbank.

Three years after that, in October of 2015, Disney Studios finished the renovation of Walt Disney's office, complete with every book and belonging that was in the office during the days he was there. Disney's office had a front room for meetings, and a back office with a kitchen. On the wall of the back office is the 4' x 4' working diagram for the design of Disneyland. When the renovation of the office was complete, Disney's piano was moved from the archives to its original place in the front room of his office.

Snow White's Piano

YOU MIGHT THINK OF THE FILM *SNOW White and the Seven Dwarfs* as just one of many feature length animations from Disney, but in fact it was ground breaking. Prior to *Snow White*, animations were limited to short and somewhat primitive comic productions. No one had ever before made a high quality color feature length animation, and no one had ever tried to incorporate the element of drama in an animation. Even at the premier showing of *Snow White*, Walt Disney was still unsure if the audience would become emotionally involved with an animated character. It was a huge relief to Disney when the first audiences loved the film.

The movie premiered in December 1937, and it went into distribution in 1938. Its original run netted more that any movie up to that time, prior to the making of *Gone with the Wind*. Up to the present day, *Snow White* is one of the greatest grossing movies of all time. Disney used much of the profits of the original release of *Snow White* to build the Disney Studios that are still operating in Burbank, California. The studio campus encompasses fifty-one acres, and is comprised of numerous buildings.

Even now after all these years, the quality of animation

produced in *Snow White* seems completely modern and of similar quality to many of the more recent Disney feature films. Yet, animation of that quality had never been accomplished before. One of the inventions that made it possible was a camera invented just prior to the production of *Snow White*. Essentially, it is a camera with framing structures located at three different distances from the camera. Animations could be placed in these frames at all three distances, so that the camera showed greater depth, making the drawings seem three-dimensional. This camera can still be seen on display at the Disney archives in Burbank.

For the voice of *Snow White*, Disney hired Adriana Caselotti, an 18-year old girl who was singing in MGM productions at the time. She was paid a one-time sum of $970. For decades after performing in *Snow White*, she was known to have made only a few uncredited performances, and several promotions for Disney to publicize re-releases of *Snow White*. In later years, she did make some public appearances, notably with Julie Andrews on her TV program in 1972.

One of the most memorable songs from *Snow White* was, "Someday My Prince Will Come." It has been ranked by the American Film Institute as the 19th greatest song ever produced in movie history. The only other Disney song to rank higher was "When You Wish Upon a Star", from *Pinocchio*, which ranked 7th.

Ms. Caselotti had an adopted son, and in 2012 he called me to schedule a tuning for the piano that he had inherited from his mother. He was living in Hollywood at the time. The piano was a 1960 Weber, made by Aeolian Weber Corporation. It was a small grand piano with a special edition case. The finish had a bluish tint, and the key cover was an unusual design. Ms. Caselotti's son was kind enough to show me some of his mother's personal photo memorabilia. One image showed her in costume playing her piano while two people in dwarf costumes stood at the far end of the piano. That photo was used as one of the promotional pieces for a re-release of the film.

Adriana Caselotti made a great contribution to the world of music and animation, and she will always be remembered as the talented singer who portrayed the beloved character of Snow White. She earned a star on the Hollywood Walk of Fame in 1987, and in 1994 she was named as a "Disney Legend," making her the first female singer and voice actor to receive that honor.

It was a privilege to meet Adriana Caselotti's son and to tune the personal piano of the original Snow White. I'm thankful for the tremendous contribution that she made to the world of music, film, and animation.

My Best Day Tuning

AFTER HAVING TUNED PIANOS FOR FORTY years, I found that my priorities had gradually changed. For example, instead of trying to get out the door quickly after a tuning, I am more often taking extra time during a service call to explain to my clients and/or their children how a piano works. I will typically invite them to ask me any questions they might have, in hopes that the information in my answers may increase their interest in practicing and playing the piano.

Sometimes I'll explain to my clients how the action escapement mechanism works, so that they can understand and appreciate what a breakthrough in design it was compared to previous instruments. The escapement mechanism is what causes a piano hammer to strike a string, then rebound away from the string, allowing the string to vibrate with enough volume to fill a concert hall with sound. Prior to the invention of the escapement action, a previous instrument, called a clavichord, had keys that propelled a "tangent" up to block against the strings, producing a sound so soft that it could be used only in a small room. The invention of the escapement action is what allowed the piano to become a concert instrument. The escapement mechanism is relatively complex, requiring ten major and numerous minor adjustments in order for it to work properly. If children are present when I'm working on a piano action, they are frequently very interested in what I'm doing, and they often want to become involved and help out.

One December afternoon as I was preparing to work on a client's piano, I asked the mother who the pianist was in the family. The mother said that it was her daughter, Emily, a 6-year old girl who was sitting nearby on the couch next to their Christmas tree. I said hello to her, but she did not respond. I went ahead anyway with offering my usual invitation for her to watch while I tuned, and I let her know that she could ask me questions, too, about the piano if she wished.

I evaluated the piano's condition, and I could see that it needed quite a bit of work. Besides a regular tuning, it also needed a "pitch raise," and a "lost motion regulation." Emily was still sitting on the couch saying not a word, so I explained to her that I would be working on the piano for a couple hours, and again I said that I would be happy to have an excuse to take occasional breaks by answering any questions she might happen to have. Emily still did not reply. Rather, she got up, left the room, and went off to play with her older brother. As I was working, I noticed that a repeated pattern emerged: Emily's brother would tease Emily until she became upset and told him to quit it. Then the mother would jump in and send Emily to her room temporarily for not playing nicely with her brother.

After the third time that this happened, Emily walked by the piano, and I decided to invite her to play a couple of keys and watch the hammers move. She was interested, but she was very hesitant at the same time, so after a couple moments she ran off again. However, she continued to come back repeatedly, and each time she stayed for slightly longer periods of time. As time went on, she seemed to be a little more open to conversation with me, so I thought I would attempt to explain the piano mechanism to her. I was careful to just glance at her as we spoke, until she became more comfortable with short interactions with me.

I finished the rough tuning and started the lost motion regulation. Lost motion regulation is a common maintenance procedure that corrects for wear on a piano action. Various pieces of felt and buckskin get compressed with use, so a technician turns a capstan screw on the back of each key until the action is working properly.

By now, Emily was feeling more at ease and she was sitting next to me on the piano bench watching me work most of the time. After I had adjusted about 60 of the 88 keys, I asked her if she wanted to adjust one key. Much to my surprise she said she would. The piano was a spinet style, whose capstans were so inaccessible that it required me to pull each key out of the piano in order to adjust it. I handed Emily a key and a capstan wrench, and without any instruction from me she turned the capstan counterclockwise one-half turn, exactly as I had been doing. I put the key back in, checked that it was regulated properly, and reported to Emily that she had done it perfectly the first try. She smiled, and she looked quite pleased.

After she did a few of these, I invited her to pull out a key herself, rather than have me do it. She removed the key carefully, exactly as I had, so as not to damage the key bushings. After she adjusted each capstan, I replaced each key, as that is a trickier procedure that risks damage to the key bushings. After she had completed a few keys in that manner, I felt comfortable enough to invite her to put the keys back in after she had adjusted them. This was not an easy procedure for a child to do, but she did it perfectly. I told her how well she was doing, and it was evident that she was feeling very proud of herself. Next, I taught her how to check if the capstan was turned the proper amount. Surprisingly enough, she figured out on her own that she should turn the capstan clockwise if it was too high. She continued working alongside me, and she regulated the last half of the bass section all by herself.

Over the years, I have taught a lot of people various tasks, and I know from experience that people usually need to hear things 3-5 times before they can actually grasp an instruction. I was very impressed with Emily's intelligence, because I couldn't recall ever meeting someone who could learn things so quickly. I never had to instruct her more than once in any given task, and it was evident that she had learned most of the procedures simply by watching me, before I had even explained to her how to do it. She was brilliant. By the time she had finished, she could easily have a conversation with me, and look directly into my eyes, too. On top of that, she was smiling happily because she was so proud of herself. Having gained an entirely new outlook, she went skipping into the next room and asked her dad if she could help him do anything.

During the course of the day, I had taught Emily about the trick question, "What is the middle note on the piano?" Before leaving, I quietly prepared the mother that she was going to be asked a trick question by Emily, and

I asked her to play along. When Emily asked her mother to choose the middle note on the piano, the mother answered, "Middle C." Emily was able to show her mother that a piano has an even number of keys, so technically there is no middle note, and the two of them laughed together. At that moment, I felt as if I could put a finger aside of my nose, and up the chimney I'd go!

After I was paid, Emily asked if I was leaving. When I responded that I was on my way, she exclaimed, "No!" It was not expressed as a tantrum. It was just an outburst of genuine disappointment. It was very sweet. I thanked her, and told her that I greatly enjoyed working with her, as well. I said that I usually have to work alone, and that it is much more enjoyable for me when someone visits with me and shows an interest in what I do.

It wasn't until a few days later that I gained the perspective to realize that it had been one of the most enjoyable and satisfying days of tuning of my entire career. In retrospect, maybe my contribution wasn't as significant as I had imagined. However, it makes me feel very pleased to think that my actions may have helped a family feel a little closer, and may have helped a little girl feel happier and more proud of herself.

THE LEGENDARY
HAL HOLBROOK

I N AUGUST OF 2015, I TUNED FOR HAL HOL-brook, the famous American film and stage actor. I had tuned for him once before, five years previously, but I didn't have the opportunity to meet him at that time. That is typical whenever I tune for celebrities, because I am usually hired and greeted by their personal assistant, rather than directly by the celebrity. When I arrived this time, Mr. Holbrook's assistant explained that they had hired a different tuner in the interval since I had tuned the piano five years ago, but they were not happy with his work. I was pleased that they decided to call me again.

In case I was to have an opportunity to meet Mr. Holbrook this time, I was all prepared with what I was going to say to him. I was planning on telling him that I saw him play Mark Twain when I was a college student in Virginia in 1967. I would explain that the college admitted only European-American students at that time, so Mark Twain was considered a pretty controversial figure, given his opposition to slavery. I hoped that Holbrook would find that amusing.

Hal Holbrook was best known for his one-man show, which he had created when he was a young man. His first solo performance was at Lock Haven State Teachers College in Pennsylvania in 1954. It was called *Mark Twain Tonight*. He would dress up in costume, complete with white hair wig and mustache, and portray Mark Twain, telling the same types of stories that Twain would have told in his day, and reciting excerpts from Twain's books with an emphasis on his comic writings. Just as Mark Twain would have done during a performance, at one point Mr. Holbrook, while seated, put his chin down so that he appeared to have fallen asleep. After a few moments, he raised his head with a start, and said to the audience, "Oh, are you still here?"

Mark Twain had done shows like this in his later days in order to raise money. He had always lost money on bad investments, so although he was the most famous person in the world in his day, he was always struggling to have enough money. It was a brilliant idea that Hal Holbrook had, to play the most popular person of an earlier era. It spring-boarded his career. He was awarded an Emmy for it, and for decades he played numerous characters on stage, on television, and in the movies.

As good fortune would have it, this time when I went to tune his piano, Hal Holbrook was sitting in the living room, relaxing on the sofa. He still had the same big shock of white hair, just like Mark Twain's. He looked a bit more elderly, but his powerful presence and gentleness were apparent in an instant. His assistant introduced me to him, but Hal didn't seem to understand who I was, because he was now very hard of hearing. I explained in a very loud voice that I was the piano tuner. He stood up and looked me straight in the eye, up close, and then he shook my hand. He said, "Oh, okay. We're going to have a famous opera singer here to perform soon. Be very careful moving the pictures of my lovely wife that are on the piano." I assured him that I would be careful with the pictures of his wife, Dixie Carter, the well-known singer and actress. Due to Holbrook's hearing loss, it was quite difficult to communicate with him, so I decided not to pursue having my prepared conversation with him.

He soon left the room, and I was ready to begin working. The piano was in the middle of the living room. Behind it, at the back of the living room was a picture window with a striking view of the San Fernando Valley. His house was on a hill above Mulholland Drive in Beverly Hills, and the view made you feel like you were sitting on a high cliff overlooking the entire valley. I could also see a big swimming pool and patio area off to the right, which was no doubt used for their family gatherings and celebrity parties.

His piano was a seven-foot Steinway, which is designated as a model "B". I checked the pitch in order to determine how much tuning I would need to do. The pitch was way above even A-442, which is the highest a piano is usually tuned. Since an opera singer would be singing with it, I decided it was worth the extra effort to bring the pitch down to A-440 (standard pitch). The reason I did that is that opera arias are usually written at the top of a singer's range, in order to show off their voice. If I had tuned the piano at the extra high pitch, it would have been a strain for the singer to sing higher than she needed to.

I tuned the piano, and everything seemed to be working properly with the piano action. I tested the pedals and they seemed to be working fine, too. Then I played

"Love is Here to Stay," written by the Gershwin brothers. I discovered that there were several notes in the mid-treble that did not function properly when the sustain pedal was depressed. I was surprised, since all the notes worked fine when I tuned the piano. I tried the notes again without the pedal and checked the most common adjustments, and they all worked fine. However, when I depressed the sustain pedal, some of the keys went down only seven-eighths of the way before something mechanically stopped them. More force was required on those keys in order for the hammers to reach the strings, which made the action uneven. When the force required to depress keys is not the same from key to key, it becomes very difficult to play a beautiful line of music.

I had worked on pianos for forty-three years at the time, and I had never seen this problem before. Since the piano was to be used for a performance, I knew it had to be fixed. My problem was how to give an estimate for fixing something I had never seen before, especially when I was not convinced that I could correct it. I decided to go forward with correcting the issue, even if I was not paid for it. Either way, I needed to know what it would take to repair it.

Since the action worked fine by itself, and the dampers worked fine when the pedal was depressed, I concluded that it had to be something in the interaction of the keys and the damper under-levers. I tried shining a bright light in behind the action as I played the keys with the pedal depressed, but I could not see anything unusual in the limited space that was visible. I pulled the piano action out millimeter by millimeter to see if it would work correctly if the action were repositioned slightly, but the system still malfunctioned even with the action out a half-inch. I pulled the action out and put it on top of the piano, and checked the function of the notes again, and they were fine. I cleaned the key bed and watched the damper mechanism work as the pedal was depressed. Everything looked normal. I repeated the above steps 3-5 times, putting the action in and out each time. I had spent 45 minutes by that time, and I was getting worried that I would not find the cause of the problem. The only thing that I could see which was unusual was the design of the piano damper tray.

All pianos have a rail underneath the damper under-levers. As the sustain pedal is depressed, a pitman (vertical rod) raises that rail, and the rail lifts all the dampers uniformly, allowing the sound to sustain. Steinway's design is different. In a Steinway, the pitman lifts not just a rail, but the entire tray, including the damper under-lever flanges, where the under-levers hinge. The result is a change of leverage, so that the whole damper assembly is lifted, except for the damper stop rail. The damper stop-rail is what prevents the damper under-levers from going too high. Since the damper stop rail stays in the same place, and everything else rises, this effectively lowers the damper stop rail. If that rail were set too low, then the travel of the keys would be limited, which was exactly the problem. I put the action back in, depressed a black key, and the damper stop rail did not allow the damper the extra 1/8" of vertical movement that it should have had. I depressed the pedal, and it was even worse; the keys could not be depressed completely. I had found the problem. I pulled the action and adjusted the damper stop rail properly, and the action worked perfectly.

In hind-sight, the cause of the problem could have

been found more quickly, if I had experienced this problem before. I could not watch the keys malfunction, because I could not see inside the piano when the action was in place. Also, with normal wear on a piano, the damper stop rail becomes loose and is pushed too high, rather than too low. The only way it can become too low is for a tuner to adjust it improperly, and then fail to test it after making the adjustment, to see if there was a problem.

For over forty years, people have asked me if it is important for a piano tuner to be able to play the piano, and I have always said, "It helps, but it usually is not a requirement." After doing this job, though, I changed my mind about that answer. If I had not played a piece of music on this piano, I would not have noticed the problem.

After completing the work, I thoroughly checked the piano over. Since it was such an unusual repair, and I had not given an estimate prior to the work, I decided not to charge Mr. Holbrook for my time. Also, I had learned a lot, and that knowledge would be beneficial to me in the future if I were ever to see this problem again.

I wrote up a bill for the tuning to leave with Mr. Holbrook's personal assistant. I hesitated for a few moments, and then I decided to write a short note to Hal on a separate piece of letterhead, since I was unable to talk with him that day. I wrote:

Dear Mr. Holbrook,

It was a pleasure meeting you today. I was a student at the College of William and Mary in 1967 when you performed *Mark Twain Tonight*. I still remember the performance, and I really enjoyed it.

I hope you and your wife are pleased with the music of the piano.

Best wishes,
Ned Klein

The following day, I arrived home late because I had a full day of tuning pianos at California State University Northridge. I needed to unwind a little, so I thought I would sit down at the computer and do a search for Hal Holbrook on the internet to read about his career. He was far more accomplished than I had realized. I did not know about his receipt of a Tony, an Oscar nomination, an Emmy, or of his numerous TV and movie roles. I checked his age, and I found out that he was 90. Then, I read that his wife, Dixie Carter had passed away five years previously. I had no idea, and now I was worried that I may have offended him by writing, "I hope you and your wife are pleased with the music of the piano." Dixie Carter spent most of her career as a singer, but she was best known for the character she played in a TV sitcom called *Designing Women*. The internet article also said that Hal would occasionally appear on the show to play her love interest.

I sat there feeling somewhat bewildered, but I snapped out of it when my phone rang. When I answered the call, I heard, "Hi, this is Hal Holbrook" in a voice clear and strong as ever. I was pretty shocked that Hal Holbrook would be calling me. I told him I was very happy to hear from him. He said he wanted to thank me for the good work on the piano and for the note that I had left for him. He said that the note, "really took me back." I explained that I didn't want to bother him yesterday as just another admiring fan, but that I did want him to know how memorable his performance was to me. He thanked me, and he told me that his wife had loved that piano. He also said, "She's passed on now. I don't know if you knew that," and I told him that I was sorry to hear that. He did not seem at all offended, as I had feared, about my saying that I hoped she would be pleased with the piano. He could not have handled it more graciously.

I let him do most of the talking, while I listened attentively. He told me that his son was dating an opera singer in New York now, and they were coming to visit soon. He explained that the piano tuning I had done was in preparation for her to perform for a few friends. He also mentioned a couple of times that his daughter would be inheriting the piano. He apologized for not visiting longer while I was there, and said that he was in the middle of something. I told him that I would love to visit with him the next time I tune the piano, and that I would be pleased to show him how everything works on the instrument. He thanked me, and we said good-bye.

My lasting impression of Hal Holbrook is one of a very gracious person, and he's definitely someone that I am very pleased to have met.

A Night With
the Vancouver
Symphony

I N THE SPRING OF 2014, I WAS SCHEDULED TO
tune for a major concert at the Younes & Soraya Naz-
arian Center for the Performing Arts in Northridge, CA.
The center, known as "The Soraya," is a large concert
hall located on the campus of California State University at Northridge. The center has two nine-foot Steinway
pianos, one voiced brightly for solo and concerto performances, and one voiced more softly for ensemble work.

The Vancouver Symphony Orchestra was on tour at
the time, and they were performing the Grieg *Piano Concerto* with Jon Kimura Parker playing the piano. I was hired
to tune both of the Steinway pianos for the rehearsal, so
that Mr. Parker could have the option of choosing which
one he preferred. The Soraya also hired me to attend the
rehearsal, to tune the chosen piano again just before the
performance, and to attend the performance as well. I was
given a second ticket for my fiancée, so she was able to
join me during the performance. A tuner is often paid to

attend a major concert, just in case something goes wrong with the piano. Early on in my career, I had found it quite stressful to sit through a performance while worrying about the possibility of a problem, but by now I felt more confident and more at ease, so I was able to just relax and enjoy the concert.

The pianist performing that evening, Jon Kimura Parker, is a well-known figure among concert pianists. He has played with major orchestras around the world. Between concerts, Mr. Parker has always found time to do interesting activities, such as touring the most northern provinces of Canada to bring classical music to remote areas. He also has a great sense of humor, recording compositions by Peter Schickele, the Mel Brooks of classical music. Mr. Parker has also been a committed educator, having taught at major universities.

During the early afternoon hours on the day of the concert, I tuned both pianos and I also checked to make sure the pedals and all of the notes were working properly. While I was busy tuning, the manager of the Vancouver Symphony stopped by, introduced himself, and asked for my business card. He looked at my card immediately and said, "Oh, great, you're an RPT." That's just what he was looking for, so that he could be assured that I was competent to prepare the piano for the high level of performance needed. RPT is the abbreviation for "Registered Piano Technician," and he knew that it's a certification awarded by the Piano Technicians Guild to technicians who have passed numerous hours of testing on the construction, tuning, regulation, and repair of pianos.

After the pianos were tuned, I had a short wait until Mr. Parker arrived. He was remarkably easy-going and friendly, especially compared with most performing artists, who would often be pretty stressed at that point of the day. After a brief introduction, he sat down and without even warming up, he launched into the dramatic fortissimo opening of the concerto on one of the pianos. He played each piano for a few minutes, and then he chose the one we had designated as the "Concerto" piano, since it has a brighter tone that could carry over the volume of an orchestra.

The orchestra was not present during the rehearsal. Apparently, they had played the piece so many times on the tour that they did not need to rehearse. The only reason Mr. Parker was rehearsing was that every piano is different in touch and tone. In addition to choosing which instrument he preferred, he needed to acclimate himself to the characteristics of that particular piano. He continued practicing various passages of the concerto for about half an hour. When he finished rehearsing, he said the piano was fine, but he asked me if it was possible to make the tone a little brighter in the high treble. I told him that I would do my best.

I began working on the piano. While I had the keyboard and action pulled out, the music director of the symphony, Bramwell Tovey, walked by and stopped to introduce himself. I felt very honored. I've never had a conductor do that in all my years of tuning. Among other awards, Mr. Tovey has won an Emmy for a classical recording, and a Juno Award for composition. Juno Awards are presented annually to Canadian musical artists to acknowledge their artistic achievements.

Also, with the Vancouver Symphony, Tovey had recently recorded all the national anthems that were needed for the medal presentations at the Winter Olympic Games in Vancouver. A few weeks after this evening's concert, he would play piano and conduct *Rhapsody in Blue* at the Hollywood Bowl with the Los Angeles Philharmonic. Mr. Tovey is a big player, yet I found him to be very friendly and relaxed. This was a very unusual group of classical musicians. Clearly they were fully confident that they could handle the performance, and they all loved their work. Their outlook seemed more like they were on holiday than presenting such a demanding performance.

After I finished working on the piano hammers, I tuned the piano again. At that point I didn't have time to go home to pick up my fiancée, so she drove over to the hall and we went out to dinner before the concert. We arrived at the hall about 20 minutes early, and we were escorted to some of the best seats in the house. Our seats were halfway back in the orchestra section just behind the crossing aisle, so we had a great view.

We had a wonderful time that evening, and the performance was absolutely beautiful. The Grieg *Piano Concerto* is now one of my favorite concertos.

PETER NERO PLAYS "GERSHWIN IN HOLLYWOOD"

THE SORAYA IS A VERY ACTIVE PERFORmance center, so I tuned there for several concerts per month for a number of years. One particularly interesting concert was held in November, 2015. I was scheduled to help Peter Nero choose which of the two Steinway pianos he would like to play, and then I would tune it for his "Gershwin in Hollywood" concert. The concert would consist of Gershwin songs which had been written for movies. Nero would be performing with a stand-up electric bass player and a female singer, so either one of the pianos would be appropriate. I had spoken with him over the phone earlier in the week, and his primary concern was that the piano have a light action. The brightness of the piano's tone was of secondary concern to him. One of the pianos, which was designated the "concerto" piano, had a lighter and faster action than the other, so that would most likely be the piano he would choose.

The Soraya is located on the campus of California

State University Northridge. I was also employed as the tuner for the music department of the college at that time, so I had scheduled tunings for various recitals and concerts at the college on the same day that I was to meet with Mr. Nero. Since the music department is located near The Soraya, I could easily walk between the two. My meeting with Mr. Nero was on a Friday afternoon, and the concert would be the following evening, on Saturday.

I had learned from experience that it's important for me to read about artists and celebrities ahead of time on the internet, so that I could be fully prepared for anything that might come up at the meeting, related to the performer's life and career. I found that Mr. Nero was regarded as one of the world's top pianists in the 50's, 60's and 70's. He had received 2 Grammys, recorded dozens of albums, and he appeared on the Ed Sullivan and Johnny Carson shows numerous times. He was presently 81, having been born in 1934.

I also read that in 1951 when he was 17, Nero played on TV with Paul Whiteman's Orchestra. I was familiar with Whiteman as a result of having read Gershwin's biography. Paul Whiteman promoted himself as "The King of Jazz" in the 20's and 30's. He hired outstanding musicians, and he was a great promoter of American music. In 1924, Whiteman had rented the Aeolian Music Hall in New York City, and invited a number of prominent American composers to debut their new compositions at his "Experiment in Modern Music." Most of the music was not particularly memorable, until George Gershwin stepped out and played the piano with the orchestra for the premier of *Rhapsody in Blue*. The *Rhapsody* was an immediate sensation, greeted by five curtain calls. Gershwin reportedly wrote *Rhapsody in Blue* in five weeks in order to make the deadline for the performance. As a result of scheduling this premier performance, Paul Whiteman had an important role in the creation of one of the finest pieces of music ever written.

Whiteman was near the end of his career in 1951, when Nero played with him, and Nero was just 17, so by 2015 it was likely that Nero was the only living person to have played with Whiteman.

When Nero arrived for our meeting at The Soraya, I was surprised at how fragile he seemed. He walked slowly, and he explained that his low back was giving him a lot of pain. He attributed it to the stress of preparing this program of Gershwin music, much of which he had never performed before. I was impressed by the courage it would require to undertake such a feat at his age. When he sat down at the piano, however, all his frailty disappeared as he played sections of the *Rhapsody in Blue* so that he could compare the speed of repetition of the keys on each of the pianos.

The two pianos to be tested had been placed on the stage next to each other, so Nero could move easily from one to the other. While he was trying out one piano, an old friend of his was sitting on the bench of the other piano, and they would talk intermittently. Nero was trying snippets of different pieces. After playing one short phrase, he turned to his friend and said, "Name that piece". When his friend couldn't name it, Nero said, "The Grieg," meaning the Grieg *Piano Concerto*.

Then, Nero played the main theme of the Grieg concerto, and his friend immediately played the answering phrase on the other piano perfectly in time. Following that, Nero played the next piano phrase and his friend played the answering phrase. His friend stole a look at me out of the corner of his eye, and he grinned when he saw my look of amazement that they could do such a thing on the spur of the moment.

After a few more minutes of playing, Nero chose the "concerto" piano, and he asked my opinion. I said, "You don't have to work as hard to play that piano. The tone is brighter and the action is lighter and faster."

He said, "Yes, it plays itself. I don't even need to be here."

If I had been thinking quickly, I could have said, "If it only tuned itself, we could both go out for dinner."

With the choice of the piano being all squared away, Nero wanted to visit with his friend, and they included me in the conversation, as well. They talked about times they would go out to lunch with Victor Borge, and the pranks that he would pull. I took the opportunity to ask him about Paul Whiteman. I told him I had the impression that Whiteman was more of a self-promoter than a great musician. I asked Nero if he agreed. He said, "I was very young at the time. Whiteman certainly hired the absolute best musicians, and he had a great ear for voices. He's the one who gave Bing Crosby his big break, and several others, as well. Many of his instrumentalists had been with him for decades. Most importantly, he was the one who rented Aeolian Hall and premiered the *Rhapsody in Blue* in 1924." Nero's friend chimed in just then, naming a list of the celebrities and great musicians who had attended the debut, including Sergey Rachmaninov, Jascha Heifetz, Igor Stravinsky, and John Philip Sousa. Nero continued, "You know, I've searched for years, and I could never find out what happened to Aeolian Hall. They must have torn it down, or something."

I turned to Nero and said, "You are a bridge to an era that the rest of us can only imagine." He nodded that he understood my appreciation. I excused myself so that Nero could continue rehearsing, and I went off to tune two more concert pianos at the college.

The next day on Saturday morning, I tuned the piano for Nero at 9 am, and the manager told me Nero was requesting that I tune it again after rehearsal in the afternoon. I rearranged my schedule so that I could arrive at 5 pm to tune the piano again. It is very common to tune a concert piano before rehearsal and then again the same day before the performance, since that's what it takes for a piano to be perfectly in tune for a performance.

Between the two tunings on Saturday, I decided to do a quick internet search for "Aeolian Music Hall, New York." An entire history of the building, the hall, and its most famous performance came up, complete with pictures and advertisement posters from 1924. I discovered that the building still exists, and it is now a school of optometry. I copied the information and printed it out so that I could give it to Nero.

I arrived at 5 pm, as the rehearsal was just ending. Mr. Nero's back was still restricting his movement, so I helped him take the ream of music off the piano and put it into his case so he could arrange everything in order prior to the concert. I also gave him the print-out from the internet about the location and history of Aeolian Music Hall. He looked at it immediately and said, "I know right where that is. It's just west of Fifth Avenue. Thanks a lot." He was quite excited about it. I imagined that it would be a pilgrimage for him if he were to go visit it.

So that he could rest before the performance, he got

up to leave the stage and I said good-bye to him. I tuned the piano, and then I requested that the manager ask Mr. Nero if he would like to check the piano tuning before I left. The manager returned to say that Mr. Nero answered that he did not need to check the tuning, so I headed home to dinner.

It had been a great thrill for me to have spent time talking with Peter Nero, and I was very happy that I was able to provide him with the Aeolian Music Hall information that he had been wondering about for so many years. Recently, I checked to see what piece of music he played with Paul Whiteman on TV in 1951, when he was 17. It was *Rhapsody in Blue*.

Sometimes Things Get Complicated

I RECEIVED A CALL FROM A NEW CLIENT, Marian, who lived in an upscale area of Hollywood, called Hancock Park. She wanted her piano prepared for a concert which would be performed by a professional pianist in her home. Marian was a member of the Santa Monica-Westside Philharmonic Committee, a group of people who help raise funds for the Los Angeles Philharmonic. The committee members hold various fund-raisers for the orchestra throughout the year, and then once a year they have a sizable group meeting to install their officers for the following year. As part of their meeting, the members would hire a concert artist to play for them.

Fortunately, over the previous years, I had enough experience with this type of situation to know that I should first evaluate the piano a week or two before the concert, rather than assuming I would have enough time to get the piano in concert condition in one afternoon.

When I arrived for the evaluation, I found a 1924 Steinway model "L", a 5 foot 10-inch grand piano in original condition. Many Steinway pianos of this era have piano actions that are so sluggish that they are almost unplayable. As it turned out, this was one of them. The problem lies in a unique process that Steinway developed many years ago.

Piano actions are made primarily out of wood. Wood is used because it has tremendous strength and resilience in relation to its weight, but it has one complication. The problem with wood is that it contracts, expands, or warps with changes of temperature and humidity. When the shape of action parts change even slightly, the touch on the instrument is effected. In the 1920's, Steinway had tried to minimize those changes by coating the action parts with a liquid paraffin, in hopes that moisture would be less able to penetrate into the wood. It worked for a while; however, after a few decades the paraffin wicked down into the piano felt actions centers. There are a number of action centers for the operation of each key on a piano. The most critical action center is the one for the hammer. The action center is essentially a hinge that pivots when the hammer is pushed toward the string. The hinge pin is held firmly in a wooden flange, and as the hammer shank pivots, this center pin rotates in two cloth bushings set to a particular tolerance so that there is a slight amount of resistance.

When the paraffin enters the felt bushings, it reacts with the nickel of the center pins, creating a green substance called verdigris. The verdigris gums up the action centers so that they won't move easily. In order to resolve this issue, a piano technician has only two choices. The first is a temporary fix accomplished by replacing the center pins and removing the verdigris by reaming out the bushings to the proper tolerance. This will only last a few months, until the paraffin reacts with the new pins and gums up the action again. The second choice is to replace the whole hammer shank and flange. The problem with replacing them is that you also have to replace the hammers and regulate the entire piano action. This procedure costs thousands of dollars, and takes several weeks to complete. I knew that would be highly unrealistic, given the narrow window of time that I was working with.

The most logical and practical solution for repairing this piano in enough time for the upcoming performance would be to take an entire day to re-pin all the hammer flange action centers. This process consists of using a special tool to push out the center pin, the part which acts like a hinge pin. There are numerous sizes of pins available that a piano technician carries. A new pin is chosen which is held firmly in the wooden flange, but is not so large as to split the flange. This requires trying different sizes of pins and choosing one which is the smallest size possible, but still is held firmly.

The cloth bushings on the hammer shank must then be reamed to the exact size of the chosen pin, so that there is the correct resistance when the pieces are reassembled. It takes a reasonable amount of skill to do this, and it is a full day's work, providing the technician is working as quickly as possible. I explained to Marian the extent of the repairs that were needed and I gave her a quote for the price for the work. She gave me her approval to proceed with the job, and we reserved two days in the following week, so I would have time to do it all.

The first day's work consisted of all the repairs. Once these were completed on the Steinway, all of the keys functioned properly again. My task for the second day was to get the piano in tune.

This particular piano had the original 87-year-old strings and tuning pins. Tuning pins are held in a wooden block called the "wrest plank," or "pin-block." When that wood dries out with age, it shrinks away from the tuning pins, and the tuning pins go loose. On this piano, the tuning pins were barely tight enough to hold the required tension on the strings. Additionally, the strings were corroded. When a string is tuned, it must slide through a bearing point near the tuning pin. If the string is corroded, then it jumps through the bearing point, so that it is difficult or even impossible to get the string to stop at the point where it is perfectly in tune. The combination of loose tuning pins and corroded strings makes for a piano that is not appropriate for use in a concert, since it is difficult to tune accurately and it can go out of tune very easily. I did not know what piece of music would be played, but I had hoped it would not be something that required a lot of heavy playing, since this piano would not hold a tuning very well. The piano was far enough out of tune, that I had to tune it twice in order to get it stable at standard pitch. A third and final tuning was done on the day before the concert.

Marian invited me to the concert, and I accepted. I was sure that I would enjoy the performance, but I also thought it would be important for me to be present just in case anything were to break on the piano. After all, eighty-seven-year-old piano action parts can break at any time, and without any warning.

The concert was in the late morning, and there was time for socializing before the committee meeting. Marian graciously introduced me to a number of the members. The living room seated 60-70 people. Most were women in their 70's and 80's, but there were a few middle-aged couples, as well. The meeting took place, complete with installation of their new officers and recognition of the out-going officers, but the concert pianist had not yet arrived. I slipped outside to the street so that I could greet him and direct him to his assigned parking place. When he arrived, I introduced myself as the piano technician. He asked me what kind of piano it was, and I told him it was a 1924 Steinway model "L" in original condition. He said, "Oh, good!"

"Oh, good," I thought. If he only knew how tenuously the piano was put together. I didn't want to disrupt his confidence, though, so I didn't say anything.

He walked in, set down his belongings, walked up to the piano, and announced that he would be playing the *Sonata in B-minor* by Franz Liszt. Somehow I managed not to make an audible gasp. If I had known he was going to play that piece, I would have said at the beginning that it could not be done on this piano. The *B-minor Sonata* is considered one of the most demanding piano pieces ever written for both the pianist and the piano. It requires a piano in perfect condition, and this piano was not even close to that.

In his day, Liszt would have three pianos on stage when he gave concerts. When one piano would break, he would just move to another one and continue. Pianos in his day were a lot more fragile than modern pianos, but I still had a hard time getting that thought out of my head. I took my seat in the back of the room, and I tried my best to remain calm.

Without warming up or even testing the touch of the piano, the pianist launched into the opening of the sonata. He played spectacularly well, and somehow the piano held up fine for the entire performance. There were prolonged pianissimo trill sections in the treble that required exact tolerances on the hammer flange action centers, and they worked perfectly. There were numerous crashing sections, where he would actually rise up off the seat and come crashing down on the keyboard with all his weight, and somehow it stayed in tune. It was useful for me to find out, also, that even though the corroded strings had forced me to compromise slightly on the accuracy of the tuning, the piano sounded fine from my seat. I can't tell you how relieved I was at the end of the performance.

The concert ended after a few short encores, and I was invited to lunch out on the patio next to the pool. The pianist thanked me for my preparation of the piano, and I replied, "It was a pleasure. I really enjoyed hearing you play." I did my best to act like this was all in a normal day's work. When I reached my car, I breathed a sigh of relief, got in the car, and drove off to my next tuning.

A GIFT FROM MOM

FOR DECADES, MY MOTHER OWNED A HIGH quality vertical piano which had an excellent action, but a somewhat muffled tone. That soft tone was perfect for a singer, as it would never overpower a voice, but the piano was not much fun to play as a solo instrument. It was a nice enough piano, but somehow it just didn't speak to me.

When my mother passed away, she left me the piano. I knew that she intended to give it to me as a sentimental gift, but I had just spent four months disposing of possessions in preparation for a move from Northern California to Los Angeles, so it didn't seem at all practical for me to move her piano from Maryland to California. Even though I had the greatest affection for my mother, I did not have any sentiment towards her piano, so I decided to give it to my niece for her little girl to play.

After moving to Los Angeles and settling in, though, I had hoped that at some point I could purchase a piano of my own once again. Some months later, on a Friday evening, I picked up the Los Angeles Times and read the estate sales column for the very first time. There was an ad for an estate sale which was to be held the next day, and one of the items listed in the ad was a grand piano. Just out of curiosity, I called to inquire about the piano. As it turned out, it was a fifteen-year-old Kawai small grand piano. I asked if it had been in a bar or had been played a lot. The estate sale representative told me that it had been in a government official's home and that it had been played only once a year by a professional pianist at their annual Christmas party. Otherwise, no one else in the family used it, since they did not play. The owners of the piano had both passed away, and their son had traveled from Chicago to LA for the weekend so that he could oversee the liquidation of his parent's possessions. The price they were asking was about 40% below market value.

This sounded like something I might be interested in pursuing, because Kawai is my favorite brand of piano. The actions are very sensitive, which allows a person to play expressively, and the tone can be very beautiful when the piano is maintained properly. I asked what time the sale would open in the morning, and they told me that it would start at 9 am. After I hung up the phone, I told my fiancée about the piano, and she encouraged me to call them back to ask if I could see the piano that evening instead waiting until the next day.

When I called back, they answered that they were at the house setting up the items for sale and that we were welcome to drive over that evening. Without any hesitation, my fiancée and I hopped into the car and headed out so that I could take a look at the piano.

The house was in Baldwin Hills. In the 1950's and 60's, it was one of only a few luxury neighborhoods in Los Angeles where wealthy African Americans lived. The neighborhood was high on a hill with a view overlooking the entire city of LA. The seller was very friendly, and he was willing to tell me about the area. He said that Ray Charles had lived diagonally behind them, but it was not known if Ray had ever played this piano. He also explained that his father had been in the Carter administration, as an assistant to a cabinet member.

I examined the piano, and it was in showroom condition. I played it a little, and the tone and touch were extraordinary. I asked the seller and the estate people for some privacy, so that I could discuss the purchase with my fiancée. It was exactly what I wanted and it was at an extremely low price, but we didn't have room for it where we presently lived. We talked it over and we decided to buy it, knowing that we were moving to a larger home soon. To celebrate the decision, my fiancée sang "Moon River" as I played the accompaniment. It turned out that the estate people had been listening at the door. When the song was finished, they burst into the room saying, "You have to buy this piano! How about if we take an additional 10% off?"

"Sold!" I exclaimed. I was very excited about the purchase.

After the piano was delivered, I tuned and voiced it, and it was a joy to play. Interestingly enough, during the same week that the piano arrived, I received a check in the mail for the final dispersal of my mother's estate. After the settlement of a will, a small percentage is always saved for a few months, in case unexpected expenses or debts were to emerge. I did not know how much the check would be for, so I did a double-take when I saw the amount was within a couple dollars of the amount that I had just paid for my new piano. It seemed that somehow my mother had given me exactly the piano I wanted after all.

Over the years, I've grown very fond of my piano. My fiancée and I have had many happy hours singing songs together, and it has brought us a lot of enjoyment. Since I've always felt it was a gift from my mother, it has been all the more treasured by me. I'm very grateful, and I guess I'm a bit more sentimental than I had realized.

MAURY

MAURY WAS ONE OF MY ROOMMATES
during the time I attended piano tuning school in
Boston. At 19, he was the youngest student in the class.
He grew up in New Jersey with an older brother who
played the piano. As a game, his older brother would play
chords on the piano and quiz Maury to identify them
by ear, and tell what key they were in and what type of
chord. As a result, Maury developed a remarkable ear for
music, and he began writing his own music when he was
in his teens.

While we were in piano tuning school, he arranged
the *Star Spangled Banner* for four-part men's voices for us
to perform on July 4th at school. It didn't occur to us then
how unusual it was to have a bass, a baritone, and two
tenors in a class of 12 people. The *Star Spangled Banner* is
usually performed as a solo, so it is a relatively difficult
piece of music to arrange for four voices. Maury did it in
one afternoon.

Maury was composing even while he was in piano
tuning school, and his writing was improving all the time.
He preferred jazz, so he joined a group of young musicians
in Cambridge called, "Composers in Red Sneakers." One

evening, I attended a concert of their members' compositions at Sanders Hall at Harvard. It was exciting to see
Maury dressed in blue jeans and red sneakers, directing a
jazz orchestra.

After graduating from piano tuning school, Maury
moved to Vermont to attend college. Upon his college
graduation, he moved to Northern California where he
worked as a music teacher and also wrote music for a children's theater group. The group gained such renown that
they traveled to Russia for a cultural exchange program.

A few years later, Maury decided to audition for *Name
That Tune,* a popular television show during the 70's and
80's. The show put two contestants up against one another
to test their knowledge of songs. The contestants would
be given a clue about a song, then they would bid as to
how many notes of the song they felt they needed to hear
in order to identify it correctly. The contestant who had
bid the lowest number of notes would get the first opportunity to identify the song and win that round.

Maury's early ear training by his brother paid off. He
became the biggest winner in the history of the show. His
image was even used in advertisements for the program.
He was known for two things: one, that he would go wild
celebrating when he won; and two, for his bravado. There
were times when he would declare, "I can name that tune
in *one note!*"

On *Name That Tune*, Maury won cars and appliances
as well as trips around the world. One of the trips was a
cruise for two around South America, staying in any five
ports for as long as they wished. He took his girlfriend,
a singer, and they stopped in Rio for a couple years. To
earn spending money, he played piano to accompany his

girlfriend's singing at night clubs, and he tuned pianos by day. They even learned Portuguese, which is the local language in Rio.

I was able to keep in touch with Maury during his travels and get updates about his adventures. I was surprised to learn that there are a lot of high-end European grand pianos in Rio. The culture of Brazil is more closely connected to Europe than to the U.S. Maury was in such high demand as a piano tuner that he could not handle all of the work. He even invited me a couple times to fly down to Rio and work with him there. It was a unique opportunity and I considered it, but concluded that I did not want to go. For one, I'm not good at learning languages, and I also could not picture myself wanting to live there long-term. I was living in the Boston area at the time, and I had invested a lot of effort in building my piano tuning business. If I left for any length of time, I would need to start over again in order to build up a clientele. I had a lot of good friends in Boston, too, as well as many good connections for singing. I was very content with my life, and I had no desire to move to a foreign country.

Eventually, after Maury completed all of his world travels, he moved back to Northern California where he was offered a job teaching at a private school. He has taught music and theater there for many years, and he is a very happy man.

Maury has a rare and remarkable talent, which he has shared with adults and children alike for decades. I'm very pleased to have been friends with such a talented and enthusiastic person.

Mason & Hamlin in the Golden Age of Pianos

THE MASON & HAMLIN COMPANY BEGAN making pianos in Boston in 1881. There were hundreds of American piano companies that thrived in the late 19th and early 20th centuries, but Mason & Hamlin is one of only a small handful that still exists today. The Mason & Hamlin brand of pianos is not as well-known as it once was; however, it is a very interesting piano company.

In 2005, I was employed to tune a grand piano that had recently been purchased by Mr. Williams, a gentleman who played trumpet for the Los Angeles Philharmonic. His son, David, was excelling at playing the piano and they had replaced their upright piano with this older grand piano. They did not know anything about the brand of the piano. They only knew that their son liked playing it, so they bought it.

At their home, I found a 1923 Mason & Hamlin model AA (6'2" overall length) grand piano in exceptionally good original condition. In the 1920's, which is known as the

"Golden Age of Pianos," Mason and Hamlin pianos were often regarded as the best piano ever made. They were endorsed by some of the best-known musicians of the day, including Sergei Rachmaninoff and Yehudi Menuhin, who owned five of them. I have seen advertisements from the 1920's that actually proclaim, "Mason & Hamlin, the most expensive piano in the world." Today, among knowledgeable collectors, a 1920's Mason & Hamlin such as this one would be considered one of the most desirable pianos a person could ever purchase.

I explained all this to Mr. Williams, and he was a little surprised at my enthusiasm for his newly acquired piano. He was not sure if I was pulling his leg about the quality of the instrument, since he, a professional, had never heard of the brand. Later in the week, he decided to get an opinion from Don, the tuner at the Los Angeles Philharmonic. He told Don that he had just purchased a Mason & Hamlin grand piano made in the 1920's in excellent original condition. Mr. Williams explained to Don that I had told him it was one of the finest pianos ever made and that it was a collector's item. Mr. Williams asked Don what he thought. Don replied, "That's what I have at home."

Mr. Williams was indeed very fortunate to own that piano. Mason & Hamlin pianos were manufactured in Boston until the 1930's, so there are still quite a few of them in and around the Boston area. However, it's fairly rare to find them on the west coast, since transporting pianos was so difficult and expensive during the era in which this one was made. Since they are less common on the west coast, even professional musicians are often unfamiliar with the brand.

Back when I was working in Boston, I would tune

them fairly often. For example, when I began tuning at Old South Church, they had two Mason & Hamlin grand pianos, one that was 5'8" overall, and one that was 7'. The seven-foot model is designated a "BB". A few years later, Old South Church acquired another BB in perfect original condition. The church had purchased a 1920's Skinner pipe organ from a mid-west civic center for five million dollars. As part of the deal, the civic center threw in a 1920's seven-foot Mason & Hamlin grand piano in showroom condition. It had a rare walnut case, and it was a wonderful instrument. It was extraordinarily resonant, with a warm and rich tone, and it had a surprisingly sensitive action for a piano of that era. One day, while the organ was being installed, I was busy tuning the newly acquired Mason & Hamlin in the sanctuary. Much to my surprise, the organ workers invited me to climb up into the scaffolding about 5 floors up, where they were tuning some of the organ pipes. These organ pipes were tuned by changing the shape of a small lip on each pipe with a tool that looks like a sardine-can opener. It takes two people to tune a pipe organ. One person sits at the organ console and plays intervals, while the other person is up in the scaffolding bending the lips on the pipes until he hears the interval beating properly. There are not very many technicians who are trained to do this, so it is something that few people ever get to see or hear being done. It was quite amazing.

The original Mason & Hamlin factory in Boston eventually went bankrupt during the Great Depression. The brand name was sold to Aeolian-American Piano Company in East Rochester, New York. They produced a lesser-quality instrument until 1982, when they also went bankrupt. The Mason & Hamlin brand name was bought and sold among several investors up until 1990 when some serious piano makers purchased the brand and began producing a top-quality piano again in Haverill, Massachusetts. Their annual production of hand-made pianos is limited to 50 uprights and 300 grand pianos, emphasizing quality over quantity. The new Mason & Hamlin pianos are, once again, some of the finest pianos in the world.

Moving Forward

M S. HARRIS HAD JUST TURNED 80. I HAD
been tuning her Steinway grand piano every six
months for five years at her home in the hills of Altadena,
located just north of Pasadena, California. Her living
room was large enough to seat 35 people, so it was regularly used as a gathering place for the three different music
performance groups to which she belonged. Each group
would have a get-together at her house and the members
would play music for one another.

I tuned for her on a June day in 2010. All three groups
were scheduled to meet at her home within the next
couple of weeks. After I had finished tuning her piano,
Ms. Harris asked if she could play her piece for me, so
she could practice in front of an audience. "Just one other
person in the room makes a big difference, in terms of
preparing to manage your nerves," she said. I told her that
I understood, and that I'd be happy to hear her play. One
of the biggest perks of doing piano work is to hear my clients play their pianos after I've tuned them. I always find
it very satisfying to experience some of the music that my
piano tuning work supports.

She pulled out the sheet music for the Chopin *Nocturne*

Number 7, which I did not initially recognize. I had never heard it played live before, but I did recall that I had heard a recording of the middle section.

She prepared me by saying, "This piece isn't very well known. It starts out very dark. In the middle it gets very stormy just before the clouds part and the sun shines through in C# major." She continued, "At one time I had this piece memorized, but now I have to use the music." All I could think of was that I could never have played that piece in my life, even with the music right in front of me. It was remarkably complex, but she played it beautifully and made it become so alive that I actually began to tear-up during one part of it. To hear her play it like that at age 80 was very moving.

After she finished playing, she said, "You have to see my new kitchen counters!" She took me into the kitchen and showed me her spectacular emerald green granite counters that had just been installed in her spacious kitchen. The granite covered a big center island, and there was a large piece on the back-splash behind the stove that went all the way up to the vent. In contrast to the light maple cabinets, it was very striking. I asked Ms. Harris if she went out to the stone yard and picked out the granite slabs herself, and she said, "Yes. It was a lot of fun." I smiled, and now I was even more impressed with her tenacity.

As if remodeling a kitchen wasn't enough of a project for a woman of her age to take on, she then told me that she had just finished landscaping her back yard, too. She gave a me a quick tour, and it was exquisitely designed with stone walkways, trees, shrubs, and a variety of flowers.

After we toured the garden, Ms. Harris told me that she had promised herself that the next year, on her 81st birthday, she would perform a one-hour program for her guests, and she did indeed follow through with that. She invited me to attend, and it was a highly ambitious program, including three compositions by Chopin, five by Schumann, five by Debussy, and three by Scriabin. Remarkably, at the end of her recital she showed no signs of fatigue. It seemed evident that performing all of that music was very energizing for her. She was so happy with the event, that when she was 82, she performed an hour-long Brahms program.

Ms. Williams taught me a valuable lesson of how important it is to keep moving forward in life, and she is an inspiration to all who know her.

GETTING PAID
TO HAVE FUN

PIANO WORK IS VIRTUALLY UNIQUE, IN
that while working, a tuner often spends a few hours
in a home visiting with clients. People usually do not tell
you the most interesting thing about themselves in the
first few minutes of conversation, but after a couple hours
they tend to share a lot about themselves. I had just such
an experience one December.

When I arrived to do a tuning for one of my clients,
Mike, he welcomed me into his house and explained that he
hadn't played his piano much lately because he didn't like
the sound of it. I briefly played his piano and noticed that
it was very shrill and unpleasant sounding. We both looked
at the hammers inside the piano, and it was apparent that
they were completely worn out. Mike asked me how much
it would be to put on a new set of hammers, and I explained
that it would be several thousand dollars. I also advised him
that it would not be a wise investment to put thousands of
dollars into a worn out hundred-year-old piano.

I suggested that for a few hundred dollars, I would
tune it, "needle" the hammers to soften them, and

regulate the hammer blow distance so that he could play the piano softly and with more control. I explained that I thought this would be a reasonable investment for a piano of that age and condition. He agreed, and I began the three hour job.

I began tuning the piano, and Mike and I didn't talk much, since tuning is fairly loud and therefore is not conducive to conversation. Once I was finished tuning, though, Mike came back into the room and we started talking while I proceeded to do the remaining work on his piano. I had remembered that when I scheduled his appointment he told me he was a musician, so I asked him what type of work he did in the music industry. He said that his entire career was arranging, composing and performing, and that he also had a recording studio in his house.

As we continued to talk, he mentioned that he had been on tour with Paul Stookey for 12 years doing production, arranging and keyboard playing. I was impressed that he had worked at that high of a level in the industry. Paul Stookey was "Paul" in *Peter, Paul and Mary*. Paul Stookey was a person I've always greatly admired for his social activism as well as for his immense talent. Mike worked for Stookey when he toured as a solo act after the breakup of *Peter, Paul, and Mary*.

As we talked some more, we discovered that we had more in common than we realized. Mike was not only the same age as I, but we were also both from the east coast. Mike and his wife lived in Bangor, Maine, and he knew all about Brooklin, Maine, the wooden boat building center where my sister and her husband had lived and built wooden boats during their retirement years.

Brooklin was also where Paul Stookey retired. In 1988,

he started a non-profit community radio broadcasting station which offered diverse musical and public affairs programming. It was first broadcast out of Paul Stookey's converted chicken coop, known as the "Hen House." That station is the first place I ever heard one of my favorite songs, called "Old Fat Boat" by Gordon Bok. I told Mike about the song, and sang it for him.

As we continued with our conversation, Mike told me about his recording studio days, and how he dealt with a difficult or demanding client, whose music he had been recording. If he had a client who endlessly demanded to have their recording tweaked just a little bit more, Mike had a solution for this. He called it the "Producer's Knob." On his recording equipment, he had installed a two-inch diameter knob that was large enough to be gripped with two hands. However, inside the equipment, the knob was *not* connected to anything. If the client was dissatisfied, Mike would go over to the producer's knob and give it a careful turn and ask the client to listen again to the recording. Usually they said it was just fine after that. It worked like a charm.

We went on to share our stories and experiences, and I told him my story about Mr. Grubb that is at the beginning of this book. You may remember that Mr. Grubb retired in Camden, Maine, a beautiful coastal town that Mike knew well. He enjoyed hearing my story about Gladys Troupin and George Gershwin, as well.

We had so much fun talking that I thought only one hour had passed, but it had already been three hours! All my work was done. Mike tried out the piano and he loved the sound. By softening the hammers, I made the tone of the instrument pleasing to the ear again. I told him that

I love doing piano work, because of the satisfaction I get in improving a piano so much that musicians feel pleased with their instruments again. It's great fun for me from start to finish.

I often realize that if I had pursued some other type of work, I never would have had the opportunity to meet such interesting people and have so many enjoyable visits as I have had with such extraordinary musicians.

WORK HARD, PLAY SPLENDIDLY

I T IS RARE FOR A PERSON TO LEARN TO PLAY the piano as an adult, unless they had piano lessons as a child. The explanation is that the human brain gets relatively hard-wired in adolescence, so that it is difficult for an adult's brain to learn new complex neural pathways. Neurologists have reported that playing piano is one of the most complex neural activities that they have found the human mind to perform. As a result, very few adults are successful in learning to play the piano, unless they studied as a child. Apparently, studying as a child creates brain pathways that continue into adulthood and can be accessed by the adult who wishes to take up the piano again. Without those pathways, an adult has a very difficult time learning to play the piano.

One person who had not studied as a child was Bill, a piano tuning client of mine. When we first met, he was approaching retirement. He had wished for most of his adult life that he could learn to play the piano. He was serious in his commitment, so his first act was to hire Kelly, one of the best piano teachers in the area. Kelly typically refused to teach adult students, explaining that adults always have a good excuse as to why they did not practice their lesson the previous week. Kelly made an exception, however, and accepted Bill as his student, because he could sense the determination Bill had to practice regularly and to learn. Kelly warned Bill that for him to be successful, he would need all the support he could get, including having a piano with a sensitive touch and a pleasing tone, so that he would get the greatest reward of beautiful music for the effort that it would take for him to learn.

Kelly referred Bill to me, and I helped Bill find a first quality used grand piano to purchase. I explained to Bill that a piano will go out of tune so gradually that he most likely would not consciously notice it. As a piano goes out of tune, though, the beauty of the sound diminishes, reducing the reward for his efforts. As a result, he might gradually start practicing less, which would slow down his progress. He took my advice to schedule tunings twice a year by the calendar, rather than waiting for the piano to sound bad before tuning.

At first it was extremely difficult for Bill to learn to read music and to control his fingers to produce the tunes. His thick fingers did not bend easily, and they barely fit between the black keys on the keyboard. Although it was challenging, he refused to give up and practiced 1-3 hours a day. His perseverance paid off. There came a point when he crossed a threshold, and he began to obtain the reward of music after all of his efforts. Suddenly he could play simple tunes and have the satisfaction of creating music.

One day when I was tuning Bill's piano he told me that he was so happy about being able to play music that it would sometimes bring tears to his eyes while practicing. He loved that he could express beauty through his music whenever he wished. He said that his entire life it had seemed to him that only *other* people could do that, but now here he was making music on the piano every day. It was a dream come true for him. Each time I tuned his piano, he was very excited to play for me, so that I could see first-hand the progress he had made. His enthusiasm was infectious.

After a couple years of playing the piano, Bill had enough confidence to take the big step of playing in a student recital along with Kelly's other students, all of whom were children. It takes a lot of courage for an adult to play in a children's piano recital. Also, Bill was a very large and powerfully-built man, so there must have been quite a contrast in the appearance of him sitting down and bending over the keyboard to play, compared to all of the children who were performing.

Bill told me that when he played at the recital, he had a lapse of memory and got stuck in the middle of a piece and had to start over from the beginning. Many a child has feared that they might do that. I imagine it was a gift to the children attending the recital to remind them that what they were doing was actually quite difficult, even for an adult. Bill also made another contribution to those children that day, by letting them see that it is okay to make a mistake and start over. I think if children have less fear of making mistakes, it frees them up to try new things and to strive for greater accomplishments.

Bill also made a contribution to me, by helping me appreciate how fortunate I am to have learned to play the piano as a child. It brings me a lot of joy, that I can sit down and play the piano, expressing myself through music, whenever I wish.

YOU NEVER KNOW

THERE IS ANOTHER REASON THAT I WAS appreciative of the contribution that Bill had provided to the young students when he made a mistake during a recital. The reason was that when I was a child I, too, made a mistake in a performance. Making a mistake was not the problem. The problem was all the judgments I made about myself as a result of the mistake. I hadn't ever seen an adult make a mistake in a performance, so I did not know that it was okay. My mother always sang perfectly, and my older brother and sister always played perfectly in their piano recitals. I now know that making a mistake is simply a sign of stretching beyond what you are comfortable doing. Back then, I thought it was a devastating sign of an inferior person.

It happened like this: I was twelve years old, and had taken up the trombone to play in the school band. I had previously studied piano with an unhappy and bored piano teacher, and I had begged my parents to let me quit piano lessons. They agreed on the condition that I take up another instrument. My school music teacher recommended the trombone for me, so I started lessons. I did passably well, playing second trombone in the school band. The mistake I made, however, was not in a band performance, but in a different venue.

The situation seemed simple enough. The minister at our church also played the trombone, and the previous year he had played in a trombone and piano duet at my mother's church women's club Christmas party. The minister was sick the following year, and my mother suggested that she and I play a duet that year. No one checked the piano at the restaurant, and it was so out of tune that I could not tune the trombone to it. We tried to do the performance anyway, and it was just dreadful. I was not that comfortable performing at that age, and to have everything out of tune was so disruptive that I played badly. The trombone does not have keys like a trumpet. It is one of those instruments that you can adjust the pitch with the slide. No matter what I did, I could not get it in tune. I plugged on and got through the piece without giving up, but it was a mess. I was so upset afterwards, that I gave up the trombone.

That might have seemed like a poor result, but you never know. My parents again required that I take up another instrument. I liked listening to Joan Baez, so I took an album cover to the music store and told them I wanted to learn to play a guitar that looks like the picture on the album cover. I didn't know that Joan Baez accompanied herself on a classical guitar, instead of a folk guitar which has a slightly narrower neck. At the music store, the salesman saw the picture of the classical guitar and signed me up for classical guitar lessons. They were so much fun that I forgot all about learning to play folk guitar.

My lessons were with Ben, the instrument repair man at the music store. I would arrive for my lesson and go downstairs where he would be soldering old battered rental trumpets back together. He would put down his tools, grab a classical guitar from the showroom, and we would go up to a teaching room on the second floor for my lesson. He would play along with me on the music, and something about the experience was delightful and charming to me. I don't recall us ever talking about anything other than the music we were playing. We would just play together for an hour and a half for the price of a half-hour lesson, so he must have enjoyed it as well. Those were my favorite music lessons that I ever had. Eventually, I progressed to music that he was unable to sight-read, so he could not play along with me. At that point, he felt obligated to send me to a more advanced teacher. My parents found an excellent college-educated classical guitar teacher for me. He was a nice enough fellow and he was an excellent teacher, but I did not enjoy the lessons nearly as much as I had with Ben, the instrument repair man. I eventually lost interest and gave up my classical guitar lessons.

At the time, that might have seemed like a poor result, but maybe not. My parents again required that I take up another instrument. My mother's voice teacher, Mr. Lewis Grubb was teaching students at my mother's home studio in exchange for providing free voice lessons for her. She arranged for me to also receive free lessons and I started learning how to sing. With Mr. Grubb's instruction, I was able to get a leading role in the high school musical. During college, I sang in the choir at the College of William and Mary. After college, I resumed studying singing with Mr. Grubb, while I sang in dinner theater productions of musical comedies. It was during that time that

Mr. Grubb pointed out to me that I did not have enough talent to make a living as a performer.

One more time, that might have seemed like a poor result, but the big picture tells another story. Mr. Grubb was the one who recommended I become a piano tuner, which is one of the best things I have ever done.

It's fun to review the impact of all these events. The uninspiring piano teacher led me to take up the trombone. The upsetting performance on the trombone allowed me to see the importance of piano tuning. It also set me on a course of learning other instruments that I might not otherwise have studied. I played classical guitar for personal recreation all through college, and I did a little folk singing, as well. My favorite music teacher was an instrument repair man, which, ironically is exactly what I ended up being. If I had never kept moving on to other instruments, I might never have taken lessons from Mr. Grubb, who advised me to become a piano tuner. Tuning pianos has allowed me to make a good living in the world of music while having the flexibility to perform whenever I wished. Mr. Grubb's instruction also allowed me, as an amateur, to perform some of the greatest pieces of music with some of the best musicians in the world. I could never thank him enough.

I think mother nature has an exceptional sense of humor. She leads us down paths we could never have imagined on our own. I am remarkably fortunate to have had such guidance.

A History of the Piano Tuning Trade, Based on Oral Tradition

YOU MIGHT BE SURPRISED AT THE INTEResting history of the piano tuning profession. To understand the development of the trade, it helps to know a short history of piano making. Pianos were invented around 1700, but it took 30-50 years to get the bugs worked out, so that they played somewhat reliably.

The breakthrough in design that led to the first piano was the invention of an "escapement" action. Prior to the invention of the piano, there were three instruments that were somewhat similar to the piano. One of those was the clavichord, which had keys that propelled a "tangent" to a string where it blocked against the string. This mechanism produced a very soft sound audible only in a small room. In contrast, a piano hammer strikes a string and then rebounds away from the string, allowing the string to vibrate with much greater volume than in a clavichord.

In order for this to take place, the mechanism that propels the hammer toward the string must move out of the way, or "escape," so that the hammer can rebound from the string.

As the key is released, the "escaped" mechanism must then return quickly to its original position so that the note may be played again. Accomplishing all this requires a relatively complex mechanism which needs periodic maintenance.

Once this mechanism was perfected, though, it allowed for musical expression that previously was not possible. Notes on a piano could then be played loudly or softly, depending on the force of the key strike. This "touch-sensitive" action also made the piano superior to a second antecedent instrument, the harpsichord. When a harpsichord key is played, one or more strings are plucked by a small quill. Harpsichords have only one tiresome volume regardless of how much or how little force is applied to the key. As a result, musical expression on this instrument was limited. The harpsichord gradually disappeared during the late 18th century with the rise of the piano.

A third antecedent instrument, the hammer dulcimer, looked somewhat like a piano without a keyboard. A dulcimer player held a hammer in each hand and struck the strings to produce a sound. Variations in volume were possible, but since the dulcimer did not have a keyboard, only two notes could be played at a time. The keyboard of a piano allowed its player to produce much more complicated and interesting music than could be produced on a dulcimer. Once the piano was invented, the harpsichord, clavichord, and hammer dulcimer all virtually disappeared.

During the 18th and 19th centuries, the piano gradually became larger and louder, and there was also an increase in the number of piano strings. As a result, more complex music was written and played on them. As pianos became a solo concert instrument, an increasing level of expertise was required in the tuning and maintenance of the instrument. Over time, the specialized occupation of piano tuner-technician gradually developed.

The actual origin of the piano tuning profession was largely lost, however, until 2015, when Fred Sturm translated a book titled *The Art of Tuning,* which was originally written in French by Claude Montal. *The Art of Tuning* was the standard text for piano service in France in the 19th century. Claud Montal was a blind, self-taught piano technician who worked in Paris. He essentially invented the piano service profession, and he started a piano tuning school in 1832. Paris was the hub of piano design innovation during the first half of the 19th century, and Montal was at the center of it all, building his own brand of piano and patenting such modernizations as an escapement mechanism for upright pianos.

The second half of the 19th century saw the American piano makers taking over as the leading innovators of the piano industry. By the end of the 19th century, there were hundreds of piano makers in the United States, and numerous piano tuning schools. Piano music was the principle entertainment in the American home, and at least one child in every family of any social standing was required to learn to play the piano in order to entertain their family and guests. Piano production and it's use became widespread, and in the towns that were too small to support piano dealerships, pianos were actually sold out of boxcars on railroad sidings.

All of this changed dramatically, though, with

the invention of the radio. Suddenly first-rate musical entertainment was available in every home. Piano sales unexpectedly took a steep nose dive starting in 1922. Piano factories began laying off their workers, which resulted in many of the skilled piano builders entering the private market for tuning pianos in homes and concert halls. This resulted in a glut of piano tuners, so fewer people took up the trade.

Piano production gradually increased again until the end of the 1920's when the depression hit. Hundreds of piano makers went bankrupt. Once again, the private market of piano tuners was flooded with former factory workers. As a result, there were far more than enough piano tuners available to provide piano services for decades to come. As a result, almost all of the piano tuning schools closed down. By the 1960's, North Bennet Street Industrial School of Boston was one of only a few piano tuning schools left in the nation.

By the late 1960's, however, the tide turned once again. The growing wealth of the middle class led to increased piano sales, while at the same time the majority of piano technicians from the 1930's were now entering their retirement. Since there were relatively few people who had taken up the trade over the previous thirty years, there was suddenly an increase in the demand for piano tuners.

The playing field changed again in the late 1960's and early 1970's. Yamaha and Kawai, the Japanese piano makers, developed automated systems for making quality pianos. They began purchasing American lumber, shipped it to Japan, seasoned it for the American climate, and manufactured pianos of greater quality than most American companies.

Yamaha and Kawai shipped their pianos back to the U.S. and sold them for less than our comparable instruments. This resulted in the majority of American piano makers going under very quickly, with only the high-end American piano manufacturers surviving. Yet again, with American piano factory workers entering the private piano tuning services market, there was another surplus of tuners.

However, another change took place in the piano tuning market beginning in the 1980's. The American culture gradually shifted over the next few decades, so that young people put less value on the trades. Computers and technology became more popular as career choices.

By the 21st century, fewer young people pursued a career in piano tuning. This resulted in an increased demand for tuners once again, even while piano sales fell slightly. Whenever there is a decrease in the sales of new pianos, the need for tuners declines much more gradually due to the fact that pianos last for 60-100 years and continually need tuning and maintenance during their entire life span. Because of this, even during the great recession when piano dealers and manufacturers were on the brink of bankruptcy, most tuners were able to keep on working.

Also, rather than purchasing new pianos, many people began restoring their old pianos. Whether new or used, all pianos need regular tuning, repairs and maintenance, so nowadays there's always an ongoing, steady stream of work for piano tuners.

TUNING FOR PERFORMANCES IN SOUTHERN CALIFORNIA

I N 2015 I WAS HIRED TO TUNE A PIANO FOR A rock band at the Hollywood Palladium. The Palladium is a dance hall that was built in 1940. The Tommy Dorsey Orchestra played at the opening, with Frank Sinatra as the vocalist. The Palladium has an 11,200 square foot spiral pattern hardwood dance floor that can accommodate up to 4,000 people. During WWII, Betty Grable hosted radio broadcasts for our troops from the Hollywood Palladium stage. In the fifties, the Lawrence Welk Show was taped there every week, and in the 1960's major rock groups, including Jimi Hendrix played the venue. In March of 1980, one of the founders of rock 'n' roll, Chuck Berry danced the "duck walk" across its stage as he played and sang "Johnny B. Goode" and "Roll Over Beethoven."

When I arrived at the Palladium, I conferred with the pianist of the rock band, and then I tuned and prepared the piano for the evening performance. After completing the job, I packed up my tools, and I found my way to the side door exit. When I opened the door, I was welcomed by a gorgeous, sunny, Southern California day. I stood at the doorway for a moment and glanced down the street in one direction, and I could see a double-decker open-top red tour bus full of tourists who were taking in all of the Hollywood sites. I turned and looked in the other direction, and high up on the hill I could see the Hollywood sign. A powerful feeling of complete peace came over me, as I knew that I was doing exactly what was right for me at that point in my life.

I headed out to my next tuning, which was at the Pasadena Playhouse, designated as "America's Theater" by government proclamation. The Pasadena Playhouse dates back to the 1920's. It is a lovely old building that housed an acting school for decades. Many famous stage and screen actors of the 20th Century learned their craft there. I typically tuned at the Pasadena Playhouse for touring musicals after they completed their Broadway runs. While tuning at the Playhouse, I was able to watch the hustle and bustle of scenery being constructed and installed on stage, and I often collaborated with the touring musicians.

One thing that I truly value about my work as a piano tuner is that it requires so much concentration that I generally feel completely at peace while I am tuning. I love being around the theater, but at this stage of my life I'd much rather be working behind the scenes. I get a lot of personal satisfaction doing my work, and there is a deep and quiet joy in that.

Piano Dance

O NE OF THE MOST DELIGHTFUL PEOPLE I have known was my former brother-in-law, Bob, who was a columnist for the *Washington Star* newspaper. Two of the things I admired most about him were his intellect and his enthusiasm.

Bob's greatest passion was for sailboat racing. He did not need to purchase his own sailboat, because he was in such high demand to race other people's boats. He sailed in amateur competitions on the Severn River in Annapolis, Maryland. The Chesapeake Bay area can have very calm conditions on a summer day, so a helmsman who can sail successfully in those conditions is in high demand. If a sailboat loses headway in calm conditions, it is difficult to regain. The reason is that it takes a fairly strong wind to overcome the inertia due to the weight of the boat. It requires less wind to keep a boat moving in the direction it is going, than to start from a stopped position. If the wind dies in the middle of a race, people's sails will go limp and the boats can end up pointing in all different directions. Sometimes crews throw out anchors, so that they can stay in the same place instead of being taken by the current in the wrong direction. I remember seeing

Bob sail right through an entire fleet of becalmed boats. It looked like he was sailing a ghost ship with its own wind. The trick was that he could perceive extremely subtle wind shifts, allowing him to adjust his course, modify the sail trim, and change the crew position in the boat so that he never lost headway. His sails were always trimmed so that they could receive whatever wind was available. By observing him, I learned that success can come from perceiving subtleties that other people may overlook.

After college, I was performing in dinner theater in Wilmington, Delaware on Thursday, Friday, and Saturday nights. On Sunday morning, I would get up early and hitchhike 100 miles south to Annapolis in order to race with Bob. Sometimes I would arrive just before the starting gun of the race. Bob would sail over to the end of the pier and I would jump on the boat and we would sail over to the starting line just in time for the start. We were racing a Cal 25, which needed a four-person crew to manage the spinnaker and the Genoa sails, so it would have been difficult for the rest of the crew if I had gotten delayed and missed the start. Sailboat racing may not look that interesting when viewed from the outside, but for the crew on the boat, managing sail changes as fast as you can and strategizing how to beat your competitors, it gets pretty exciting.

One of the things that made Bob so much fun to be around, was that he figuratively danced his way through life. If we were preparing to go sailing, for example, he would say, "Let's do the sailing dance," meaning that we would gather all our gear together, preparing to go to the sailboat. Likewise, he would say, "Let's do the camping dance" if we were collecting all of our gear for that activity. By labeling an activity a "dance", he made what could have been a tedious process into something we could instead begin with a positive outlook. He would frequently say, "You just need to have the right attitude."

When I was young, and before I met Bob, I did not realize that there was an alternative to my usual mindset, which was that piano practice was tiresome and even somewhat boring. My attitude toward piano practicing not only made my life less enjoyable, but it also hurt my progress in learning to play well. If I had known then about Bob's secret of making everyday activities and challenges into a dance, I could have done the "piano dance" each day and approached my piano practice with enthusiasm and a smile.

If you are studying piano, I invite you to do the "piano dance" each day. By labeling your practice with a positive viewpoint, you may find greater joy and faster progress as you learn to play this wonderful instrument. The rewards will be great. Not only will you have the ability to express yourself through music, you will find that your ability to play the piano will open numerous doors for you throughout your entire life.

You can never predict what may happen. For example, when I first met my extraordinary fiancée, I could tell immediately that she was beautiful, witty, intelligent, creative, and compassionate. I was concerned that I could not measure up to her as far as personal attributes. We talked, however, and the conversation took a positive turn when she said, "Oh, you play piano, eh?" Her favorite thing in life is to sing. I have been around hundreds if not thousands of singers in my life, and I have never found another person who got so much pleasure out of singing just around the house. She is an amateur and is too shy to sing around anyone else, so I get to be the only one who ever hears her sing or who ever sees the remarkable joy it brings to her. I can sit at the piano in the living room and play an introduction, and she will appear in the balcony above and sing, "I Could Have Danced All Night," from *My Fair Lady*. I can't tell you how happy I get when she does that.

On other occasions we play and sing our own words to duets, such as "Sixteen Going On Seventeen" from *The Sound of Music*. For that song, we substitute our actual ages, so instead of "sixteen" and "seventeen," the lyrics become "sixty-one" and "sixty-two." Whenever we wish, we can have the joy of creating music together at home, without needing anyone else to be there.

Who could ask for more than that.